# Teaching Women's and Gender Studies

Incorporate Women's and Gender Studies (WGST) into your high school classroom using the powerful lesson plans in this book. The authors present seven units organized around four key concepts: Why WGST; Intersectionality; Motherland—History, Health, and Policy Change; and Artivism.

With thought questions for activating prior knowledge, teaching notes, reflection questions, reproducibles, and strategies, these units are ready to integrate purposefully into your existing classroom practice. Across various subject areas and interdisciplinary courses, these lessons help to fill a critical gap in the curriculum.

Through affirming, inclusive, and representative projects, this book offers actionable ways to encourage and support young people as they become changemakers for justice.

**This book is part of a series on teaching Women's and Gender Studies in the K-12 classroom. We encourage readers to also check out the middle school edition.**

**Kathryn Fishman-Weaver, PhD (she/her)** is the executive director of Mizzou Academy. In addition to this book series, she is the author of four additional books in education, *Wholehearted Teaching of Gifted Young Women* (2018); *When Your Child Learns Differently* (2019); *Brain-Based Learning with Gifted Students* (2020); and *Connected Classrooms,* co-authored with Stephanie Walter (2022). She has lectured and led professional development sessions and conferences around the world.

**Jill Clingan (she/her)** is the composition and literature lead teacher for high school students in Mizzou Academy's Dual Diploma program. This program supports high school students in Brazil who are earning both a Brazilian Ensino Médio diploma from their Brazilian school as well as a U.S. high school diploma from the University of Missouri. At Mizzou Academy, Jill has also authored two high school language arts courses, co-authored an interactive grammar resource, and serves as an administrative editor.

T0373580

# Teaching Women's and Gender Studies

Classroom Resources on Resistance, Representation, and Radical Hope (Grades 9–12)

Kathryn Fishman-Weaver and
Jill Clingan

Routledge
Taylor & Francis Group
NEW YORK AND LONDON

Cover image: © Getty Images

First published 2023
by Routledge
605 Third Avenue, New York, NY 10158

and by Routledge
4 Park Square, Milton Park, Abingdon, Oxon, OX14 4RN

*Routledge is an imprint of the Taylor & Francis Group, an informa business*

*Library of Congress Cataloging-in-Publication Data*
Names: Fishman-Weaver, Kathryn, 1981- author. | Clingan, Jill, author.
Title: Teaching women's and gender studies : classroom resources on resistance, representation, and radical hope (grades 9-12) / Kathryn Fishman-Weaver, Ph.D. and Jill Clingan.
Description: New York, NY : Routledge, 2023. | Includes bibliographical references.
Identifiers: LCCN 2022021972 | ISBN 9781032344744 (hardback) | ISBN 9781032344720 (paperback) | ISBN 9781003323327 (ebook) Subjects: LCSH: Women--History—Study and teaching (Secondary) | Gender identity—Study and teaching (Secondary) | Women's studies.
Classification: LCC HQ1121 | DDC 305.4071/2—dc23/eng/20220728 LC record available at https://lccn.loc.gov/2022021972

ISBN: 978-1-032-34474-4 (hbk)
ISBN: 978-1-032-34472-0 (pbk)
ISBN: 978-1-003-32332-7 (ebk)

DOI: 10.4324/9781003323327

Typeset in Palatino
by Apex CoVantage, LLC

Access the Support Material: www.routledge.com/9781032344720

# Contents

Support Material    vi
Acknowledgments    vii
Meet the Authors    ix

**Introduction**    1
Positionality    4
About This Book    7

1    **Why WGST?**    9
Unit 1—Feminist Theory: Introduction    21
Unit 2—We Can All be Changemakers for Justice    42
Extension Exercises for Concept 1    57

2    **Intersectionality**    60
Unit 3—Matrices and Margin    71
Unit 4—The Personal Is Political: The Power of More Complete
    Stories    86
Extension Exercises for Concept 2    103

3    **Motherland—History, Health, and Policy Change**    105
Unit 5: Policy Change    114
Unit 6: Maternal Health    136
Extension Exercises for Concept 3    158

**Proseminar: Artivism**    162

**Epilogue**    174

Glossary    177
References    189
Index    204

# Support Material

The handouts in this book are also available on the book product page online, so you can easily print them for classroom use. To access these downloads, go to www.routledge.com/9781032344720 and click on the "Support Material" link.

# Acknowledgments

We are grateful for the young people we work and learn with. Their vision, leadership, and radical hope that the world can be more just, inclusive, and vibrant inspires and fuels our work.

We also want to thank each other. From shared desserts (that crème brûlée in São Paulo), to book recommendations (so much poetry), to service projects addressing food insecurity in mid-Missouri, to eating ice cream with middle school scholars on a school roof in Brazil (dessert again), we are grateful to each other. For all our shared passions, and more importantly, all our different experiences and perspectives, we both believe the other is the right partner and co-author for this project. We also want to acknowledge our families who believed in and supported this work. The love of our spouses, our children, and our parents is evident throughout this text.

The incredible advisory editors who gifted us their time, expertise, and compassion made this book immeasurably stronger. Dr. Elisa Glick, Dr. Adrian Clifton, Dr. Dena Lane-Bonds, Stefani Domingues, and Lisa DeCastro were gracious in pointing out our blind spots, suggesting new directions, emailing important additions, sending specific notes and corrections, teaching us a better way, and offering their continued encouragement. Each of these remarkable teachers are leaders in their fields and communities. In this book, you will read section forwards and letters from the advisory editors listed above; however, these give you only a glimpse into the significant mark these five thought leaders have left on this text.

An important origin story for this project are the Women's History Month resources we developed each year. As such, we want to thank the colleagues who helped with these teaching guides and clarifications, especially Brian Stuhlman, Dr. Sherry Denney, Stephanie Walter, Lou Jobst, Anthony Lehman-Plogger, and Nina Sprouse. We are also grateful for Dr. Thitinun "Ta" Boonseng, Artitaya "New" Jantaraprapa, Dr. Shivasankalp "Sankalp" Shivaprakash, Greg Soden, Rachel Andresen, and Dr. Jennifer Fisher who sent notes and resources that broadened our understanding.

Several schools and educators were early champions of these lessons. In particular, we would like to thank Robert "Bert" Garner, Rossella Beer, and Luiza Dutra for sharing meaningful ways they implement creative and inclusive practices in their school communities in São Paulo. Additionally, we are grateful to Matheus Nucci Mascarenhas and Marília Mascarenhas for their important contributions to this book.

We are indebted to teachers who were important in our own feminist journeys. Kathryn would like to thank Dr. Barbara Bank (in fond memory); Dr. Christine Patterson; Dr. Brad Wing; and Dr. Joan Hermsen, who first introduced her to feminist scholarship as an undergraduate; and later Dr. Jeni Hart, who supported her work as a feminist researcher during her doctoral program. Jill would like to thank Mrs. Deborah Murray, Dr. Jerry Dees, Dr. Karin Westman, and Dr. Phil Nel, graduate school professors who taught her how much stories matter and who often made her think, as a student in their classes, that there was no place in the world she would rather be.

Finally, thank you (truly, purposefully) to Lauren Davis, Julia Giordano, Emma Capel, and the Routledge team for their belief in this project and for their wisdom and care in bringing it to fruition.

# Meet the Authors

**Kathryn Fishman-Weaver, PhD (she/her),** began her teaching career as a special education teacher in a public K-8 school in Oakland, CA. Since then, she has taught and led programs in special education, gifted education, English language arts, and teacher preparation. Kathryn currently serves as the executive director of Mizzou Academy. She is the author of four additional books in education, *Wholehearted Teaching of Gifted Young Women* (2018); *When Your Child Learns Differently* (2019); *Brain-Based Learning with Gifted Students* (2020); and *Connected Classrooms*, co-authored with Stephanie Walter (2022). Despite these academic publications, her first literary love is poetry, and that is a love that has lasted a lifetime. Kathryn's work has appeared in numerous publications and been referenced by the U.S. Department of Education. In addition to work in K-12 schools, Kathryn also supports the University of Missouri's teacher education program by coordinating required courses on culturally responsive, ethical, and community-engaged teaching practices. She has lectured and led professional development sessions and conferences around the world.

**Jill Clingan (she/her)** is the composition and literature lead teacher for high school students in Mizzou Academy's Dual Diploma program. This program supports high school students in Brazil who are earning both a Brazilian Ensino Médio diploma from their Brazilian school as well as a U.S. high school diploma from the University of Missouri. At Mizzou Academy, Jill has authored two high school language arts courses, co-authored an interactive grammar resource, and serves as an administrative editor. She has traveled to southeast Brazil to work with schools and lead and present at international educational conferences.

Jill holds a bachelor's degree in psychology and a master's degree in English literature. Before teaching at Mizzou Academy, she homeschooled her daughter through much of elementary school and taught writing and literature classes at Kansas State University. Additionally, Jill's work has appeared in *Practicing Families* and *Grit*. If you showed up on the five-acre spot of land where she lives with her family, you might very well find her quoting poetry to her motley crowd of dogs, cats, chickens, turkeys, and ducks.

# Introduction

> Gender equality is not only a fundamental human right, but a necessary foundation for a peaceful, prosperous and sustainable world.
> (United Nations, 2020)

Jill and I (Kathryn) work for a global school system. This work with young people and educators from around the world has informed how we think about feminisms, justice, access, and the inherent reciprocity between global and local perspectives (see pp. 25-26 for more information on global and transnational feminisms). The United Nations provides a strong foundation for understanding the global and multitude of local, landscapes related to gender and justice.

In 2010, UN Women was established to help advance and coordinate this ongoing work from within the United Nations. In 2015, the United Nations released 17 Sustainable Development Goals (SDGs). The United Nations' fifth SDG is to achieve gender equality and to empower all women and girls. There are even deeper roots in the Commission on the Status of Women, which remains the main global intergovernmental body dedicated to women's empowerment and gender justice work. Since its founding in 1946, the Commission on the Status of Women has been able to report on significant accomplishments, yet much more work still needs to be accomplished. According to reports by the United Nations (2020), women and girls continue

DOI: 10.4324/9781003323327-1

to have unequal access to resources including basic resources (e.g. food, shelter), leadership positions, educational opportunities, and safety. For example,

- Women and girls are significantly more likely to live in extreme poverty (UN Women, 2021-b).
- Women hold only 28% of managerial positions (United Nations, n.d.-e) and remain underrepresented at all levels of political leadership (UN Women, 2021-a)
- Women and girls are paid 23% less than their men counterparts—this figure is compounded for women of color (UN Women, n.d.).
- "1 in 5 women and girls between the ages of 15 and 49 report experiencing physical or sexual violence by an intimate partner within a 12-month period" (United Nations, n.d.-b), fewer than 40% of these women and girls seek help, and fewer than 10% report violence to the police (UN Women, 2022).
- 129 million girls are not in school, and less than half of primary and secondary schools have achieved gender parity (UNICEF, n.d.).
- According to the United Nations 2020 Free and Equal Report, official data on violence against the LGBTQIA+ community is difficult to collect. This is because of a lack of stable systems and legal protections for reporting crimes against LGBTQIA+ individuals. However, all analyses point to a clear pattern of widespread and brutal violence against LGTBTQIA+ individuals, which has been reported in all regions of the world (Free & Equal United Nations for LGBTI Equality, n.d.).

In what ways can the high school classroom become a site for exploring and even *complicating* these big issues. For example, as we (Kathryn and Jill) consider what feminism and gender justice mean to us, we include issues of racial justice (such as health disparities, racism, and intergenerational trauma) and LGBTQIA+ inclusion (including health disparities, heterosexism, and gender-based violence) as essential issues for gender justice in the 21st century. In teaching systemic and global issues, how can you and your class communities center humanity and hope? When educators approach global awareness from a people-centered perspective (Fishman-Weaver and Walter, 2022), they move beyond a curriculum of despair and pain (Tuck, 2009) and enter a space that is honest, difficult, and also full of hope, resistance, and joy. In these chapters we (Kathryn and Jill) celebrate the incredible ways advocates thread knowledge, innovation, and care across all sectors of industry, influence, and humanity. The following teaching units shine a light on leaders, creators, activists, and dreamers who have and are changing the world. Believing that personal stories are the shortest distance between people, these chapters honor that the cartography of oppression and resistance is as varied as a topographic map.

Yet, our collective stories, as different as they—as we—are, paint a global landscape of diversity, of beauty, of pain, of courage, and of triumph.

If you scan a university course list, you will likely find classes on Women's and Gender Studies. However, if you scan a middle school or high school course directory, such courses are far less likely. This book offers ideas, strategies, and activities to begin to fill this gap in the field and you can begin this work within the classes you already teach. Women's and Gender Studies is inherently interdisciplinary in nature. These lessons include meaningful extensions and activities in language arts, social studies, the sciences, and the arts among others. Recognizing the power of asset-based approaches and knowing that language matters, we (Kathryn and Jill) refer to the K-12 students we work with as *scholars*. The lessons included in the following chapters ask young people to engage in critical analysis; to launch action projects in their local communities; and to participate in the production of knowledge through their writing, advocacy, art, and creative works. Our own experiences with young people have taught us that they are not waiting to become scholars and leaders; instead, they are already pushing the boundaries of learning and impacting change. By choosing to use the term *scholars*, we (Kathryn and Jill) hope also to open up and expand the definition of what *and who* counts within the lexicon of scholarship. Is a 16-year-old who creates an art installation on mental health a scholar? Is an 11-year-old who launches a community-wide food drive a scholar? Is a 14-year-old who speaks to their city council about health disparities a scholar? Absolutely. As a feminist project, we do not see scholarship as only something that can happen only within a specific higher education context. Instead throughout this book, we are proud to center and honor the wisdom and scholarship that comes from the lived experiences, passion, and valued efforts of young people.

In her seminal work on literature, Dr. Rudine Sims Bishop (1990) asserted that scholars need books that serve as windows, mirrors, and sliding glass doors. We believe the same is true across all curricula. Young people need *mirrors* to see themselves, their realities, and their experiences in the people they study. They also need *windows* to meet people, realities, and experiences that are different from their own. And finally, our classrooms need *sliding glass-doors* that encourage young people to walk boldly into new realities.

Representative future-casting is important for self-efficacy. When young people look into their school curricula, do they find confident and inspiring change makers who share their identities? We (Jill and Kathryn) have written this book with a belief that young people can impact change, lead movements, and create projects that matter. Our hope is that these lessons support you in celebrating scholars not only for who they are, but also for who they can be. We (Kathryn and Jill) believe the classroom can be a powerful site for beginning this work toward justice, inclusion, and representation.

## Positionality

As with most big ideas, this project can be traced to several distinct origin moments including our (Kathryn and Jill's) separate formative and personal experiences of gender discrimination, transformative conversations we've shared with our own daughters *and* sons, and to our curriculum and teaching work in K-12 classrooms. Each of these experiences shaped who we are as feminist educators, influenced the content of this book, and informed our persistence for bringing this text to fruition.

The most palpable inciting incident is the annual series of teaching resources we release each spring for Women's History Month. These classroom activities were our first conversations with each other about what feminist teaching could be in middle and high school spaces. This thought work was important for our professional growth as educators and shaped further dialogue and decisions within our own school community. One year the series helped us launch an author audit of texts in our language arts courses, which was followed by a dramatic increase in women's voices, authors, and scholars in our curriculum. This work then led to a more intersectional approach to curricular work centered on culturally responsive choices about representation and diversity across many different identities (Gay, 2002). In addition to complicating the canon (Illich & Alter Smith, 2018) and offering more diverse worldviews across our courses, we also wanted to "anchor curriculum in the everyday lives of our scholars" (Kozleski, 2010, p. 6).

The annual Women's History Month project became both a celebration and an initiative, what my (Kathryn's) mother called "an agenda for good." Each year we aligned our resources to the National Women's History Month Alliance's annual theme. In January or February we sent out a call for proposals to our colleagues, and then we poured into the project with resolve to release it as close to March 1 as possible. We challenged the teachers in our communities to think of our Women's History Month resources as seeds that grew well beyond March. Knowing that these seeds would need what one of our colleagues calls "care and feeding," we wanted to give teachers a volume of resources they could integrate throughout the year. And so, aptly, one weekend in March, we decided to look more critically at the resources we had built out over the past several years to see if they might offer a celestial map for something bigger, something more permanent, something much like the book you are holding in your hands.

We (Kathryn and Jill) are career educators, introverts, poetry lovers, and mothers. We can map our friendship from a bookshop in central Missouri; to school events in São Paulo, SP; to deep conversations around my (Kathryn's) kitchen table, preferably with some of Jill's baked goods. We are also both White, cisgender women of European (eastern and western) descent. We recognize that our similar lived experiences limit the scope of this project. Being aware of this limitation, we strive to (1) be transparent about our own positionality; (2) intentionally work with advisors and editors who represent different identities and lived experiences from our own; (3) draw on the work of Black, Latina, Indigenous, Asian, and LGBTQIA+ scholars; and (4) iterate based on the feedback we've received implementing these lessons in global classrooms.

Across these units, we (Kathryn and Jill) are committed to teaching a multiplicity of voices. And yet, even with these commitments, there are some lived experiences that, despite study and friendship, we know we will never fully understand. We recognize that if authors from other backgrounds were writing this text, it would likely be a very different book. One system we've employed to expand the voices and perspectives in this book is working with advisory editors on each conceptual section. These editors gave us important feedback on our chapters, points to consider or clarify, and impressions on how these activities might function in their classrooms. We are grateful to the five advisory editors who each took on a conceptual section as an advisor and thought partner. These editors bring diverse identities and lived experiences to this text. They were critical in helping Jill and me (Kathryn) identify our blind spots and making this text stronger and more effective. Each conceptual chapter includes a forward by the advising editor where they share their thoughts on the concepts and activities.

While we (Jill and Kathryn) share much in common, we also have important differences that influenced the content and structure of this text.

**Kathryn Fishman-Weaver (she/her).** My grandmothers—the daughters and granddaughters of immigrants—were among my most important teachers. As a young woman, my grandma Sophie wrote for an underground newspaper in Brooklyn, studied languages at night school, and hitchhiked to national protests. Meanwhile, my grandma Norma taught in a one-room schoolhouse in Northwestern Iowa, wrote poetry that she kept mostly to herself, and shared an incredible love story with her high school sweetheart. I am deeply indebted to the strong-willed women in my family including my grandmothers, my mother, my sister, my daughter, my aunts, and soon a daughter-in-law. You can see their influence across so many of my decisions and ways of being.

In high school, I performed original (often angsty) poems in the coffee shop circuit on the main drag of my hometown in middle America. I had a close circle of girlfriends who supported me during my formative years. In college, I minored in Women's and Gender Studies and changed my major several times, finally landing on sociology with an extra minor in English writing. Soon after graduating, my spouse and I ran off to California, where I worked for a social justice nonprofit and then suddenly changed course again to become a school teacher for the Oakland Unified School District. The classroom became my home, my scholars my new instructors, and teaching my vocation. Along the way, I earned a master's degree in special education and a PhD in educational leadership and policy analysis. I have now taught nearly every grade from kindergarten through university. I've taught language arts, elementary, high school, special education, gifted education, math, finance, and teacher education. I've facilitated several research studies on gender and education, including student-led projects on the state of feminism, the lived experiences of young women during the transition from high school to college, and how the visual arts can support emotional processing. For the past six years, I've served as a director for a global K-12 school system, which is also where I met Jill.

**Jill Clingan (she/her).** I grew up with two strong women as my role models—my mom and my grandma—who exemplified strength, resilience, wisdom, grace, and faith. My grandma married her high school sweetheart and then spent the next 64 years deeply loving my grandpa, her children, her grandchildren, and her great grandchildren. She was also famous for her pies, an art I try to emulate. While in many ways she filled what appeared to be a very traditional role as a mom and pastor's wife, she also did not always bend to the norms expected of her, an art I try to emulate as well. My mom was a preschool teacher who prioritized and adored her family. She nurtured me, supported me, and passed on to me her perceptive wisdom. She also fiercely believes in me, and I carry that strength with me. Now, my daughter is part of that circle of want to emulate her courage and confidence. I am so very proud of her, and in a twist of parental role-reversal that I didn't quite expect, I want her to be proud of me, too.

I did not grow up learning feminist theory, and any feminist writers I read were by pure accident, but I was a voracious reader, and I was always attracted to women authors and books with strong women characters. Louisa May Alcott was my beloved childhood companion, and as I got older, I discovered the works of Virginia Woolf, Sylvia Plath, Alice Walker, Kate Chopin, and Maya Angelou. I had always wanted to be an English teacher, but as a senior in high school, my science teacher stopped me in the hall one day and told me I should reconsider this career path. Her words stunned me and ultimately changed the course of my life. Instead of following my dream to become an English teacher, I pursued a different educational path, but after wrestling with myself for years, I finally followed my heart and went back to school to earn a degree in my first love: English. I taught writing and literature courses at Kansas State University, and then took an unexpected detour in my educational and career path as I spent several years homeschooling my daughter. For the past six years, I have been a composition and literature lead teacher for the global K-12 program where I met Kathryn.

Our paths, as different as they are, have organically led us to a space to write this book. Kathryn and I (Jill) have worked on many projects together over the past several years, but we always come around to this space: a space to amplify the voices of women and share their stories, their contributions, their challenges, and their triumphs with teachers and scholars in the classroom. This book is more than a project for us; it is a mission of our hearts and a work of our souls. As such, it is a book that is more than two-dimensional words on a page. It is a living space for us to co-create expansive spaces in our schools, spaces that advance justice and inclusion, celebrate more complete stories, and encourage young people to engage in making the world a more just place.

## About This Book

This book is informed by feminist scholarship around the production of knowledge, the power of personal narratives, and the intersections of identity. It is deepened by the wisdom gained through collectives. These chapters both acknowledge the ways privilege and power complicate our systems and encourage radical hope that those same systems can be challenged and reimagined. Believing that "feminism is for everybody" (hooks, 2020) and that "we should all be feminists" (Adichie, 2014), this book aims to offer a text that high school teachers and scholars can see themselves and their communities in. Although we could not include photos of the 100+ key figures celebrated in the following lessons, we do encourage you to share images of the artists, activists, scientists, advocates, writers, and student leaders featured in these lessons. These key figures represent ethnic, racial, religious, gender, cultural, and ability diversity. It is our hope that the units include multiple mirrors and windows for your scholars (Bishop, 1990). Each unit is organized around three core concepts: representation, resistance, and radical hope. These concepts inform how the following chapters were developed, the voices and stories we strove to include, and how we (Jill and Kathryn) imagined agency being negotiated and celebrated in classroom spaces.

The book is structured around the following three key concepts for student inquiry plus a proseminar study on artivism.

- ◆ Concept 1: Why Women's and Gender Studies (WGST)?
  - – Unit 1—Feminist Theory
  - – Unit 2—We Can All Be Changemakers for Justice
- ◆ Concept 2: Intersectionality
  - – Unit 3—Matrices and Margins
  - – Unit 4—*The Personal is Political*, the Power of More Complete Stories

◆ Concept 3: Motherland—History, Health, and Policy Change
  – Unit 5—Policy Change
  – Unit 6—Maternal Health
◆ Proseminar—Artivism

Each concept begins with a section overview with learning objectives and guiding questions for both scholars and educators. The concepts include an activity to honor prior knowledge, two units related to the overarching concept, several lessons for exploration, and a synthesis project.

In addition to lesson content, each concept also includes a care letter for educators. Teaching is heart-heavy work. Teaching Women's and Gender Studies often taps into complicated, charged, and sensitive issues that require additional heart work. In these care letters, we (Kathryn and Jill) want you, too, to feel seen and affirmed in all you are carrying by engaging in this important content.

If possible, we recommend starting with Concept 1, which offers a foundation for Women's and Gender Studies and key themes developed throughout the text. The lessons are written in general enough terms to be accessible across the high school context. As with all lessons, you may find there are ideas, vocabulary, or activities that require more scaffolding and others that lend themselves to more opportunities for enrichment. Each unit includes a focus term and additional vocabulary supports throughout the lessons. You can also find helpful links and suggestions for extending the learning at the end of each chapter. Throughout the teaching notes are invitations and permission to make this content your own and to expand and compress lessons based on the unique needs and context of your class communities.

Thank you for your interest in bringing more Women's and Gender Studies lessons to the high school classroom. With you, we (Kathryn and Jill) share a belief that this work matters, that young people matter, and that together we can co-create a more just world.

The book you are holding is not a complete curriculum. On their own, these units do not correct for all the missing voices and histories; they do not solve global challenges. However, we hope they are seeds for this work. The book you are holding comes to life in what happens off the page, in the discussions, projects, and initiatives of you and your scholars. As the ancient Taoist proverb said, "A journey of a thousand miles begins with a single step." May these units be powerful first steps, conceptual catalysts, and inspirational sources that drive your classrooms forward to greater inclusion, action, and representation.

# 1

# Why WGST?

## Advisory Editor Concept Foreword by Dr. Elisa Glick

*Dr. Elisa Glick (she/her) is an associate professor of English and Women's and Gender Studies at the University of Missouri, where she teaches courses on feminist and queer theory, sexual and gender diversity, queer literature and culture, and 20th-century literary and artistic culture. She has published in the fields of gender and queer studies, most notably her book* Materializing Queer Desire: Oscar Wilde to Andy Warhol. *Elisa has expertise in feminist, anti-racist, and equity-focused pedagogies and is the founder of Mizzou's Faculty Institute for Inclusive Teaching. A diversity, equity, and inclusion consultant and the owner of Elisa Glick Consulting, she works with schools, colleges, and universities to help them build more inclusive and equitable classrooms and create sustainable change. Elisa holds a PhD in English from Brown University. She lives in Columbia, Missouri, with Carolyn Sullivan, her spouse and life partner of almost 30 years.*

I never set out to be a Women's and Gender Studies (WGST) Professor or a feminist theorist. But looking back on my own academic journey, I think these are the spaces I most felt at home because I was able to bring all of who I am to my teaching and scholarship. For the first time, I felt

DOI: 10.4324/9781003323327-2

welcomed into a supportive and mind-expanding community of learners, teachers, and activists who respected and cultivated difference, openness, nonconformity, ambiguity, emotion, queerness, and pleasure. This is the kind of inspiring and transformative community that *Teaching Women's and Gender Studies: Classroom Resources on Resistance, Representation, and Radical Hope (Grades 6–8)* invites us into—a brave space of connection, trust, and justice grounded in the shared learning experience of WGST teachers and students.

*Teaching Women's and Gender Studies* breaks new ground by introducing the interdisciplinary field of WGST to the K-12 classroom, providing an accessible yet conceptually sophisticated roadmap that enables both educators and young people to become change agents for justice. In their first chapter "Why WGST?," Jill Clingan and Kathryn Fishman-Weaver not only deftly introduce the major concepts, issues, and problems in the field, but they also highlight their relevance to contemporary debates about social inequalities that disproportionately impact communities of color, Indigenous peoples, and LGBTQIA+ communities in national and transnational contexts. As a tenured professor who has taught and published in WGST and Queer Studies for the past 20 years, it's clear to me young people are leading the way to radically transform notions of gender and feminism. It's therefore especially fitting that, in the chapter that follows, Jill and Kathryn recognize and honor the individual and collective wisdom of young people while providing them with the necessary tools to increase their knowledge of WGST and what it has to offer increasingly diverse Gen Z learners.

"Why WGST?" offers a thematic focus that explores both differences and shared connections between and among feminist frameworks, distilling for readers some of the most complex and important insights in the field today. One of the key takeaways for students is there is far more diversity within feminism than is commonly recognized. Disrupting linear narratives of feminist "waves" that often privilege Western, White, middle class, cishet women, the chapter emphasizes that there is no single identity for or history of "feminist," "feminism," or "Women's and Gender Studies." Although they provide definitions of influential feminist movements and theories, the authors do not primarily aim to offer a survey of different feminist frameworks. Building on the assertion of multiple feminisms rather than a singular feminism, the chapter aims to (1) demonstrate the strengths of WGST as a mode of knowledge production grounded in lived experience; (2) introduce students to gender as a socially constructed category of analysis and WGST as a discipline that uses a gender lens to deconstruct dominant paradigms; (3) examine how social inequalities and resistances shape forms of activism around the globe; (4) introduce students to contemporary feminism's most influential concept, intersectionality, a framework for understanding how multiple identities and systems of oppressions intersect; (5) increase awareness of and reflection on social location and the diverse impacts of power and privilege for individuals and communities; and (6) provide experiential learning activities so that practitioners can develop the critical consciousness necessary to become advocates and changemakers for justice. For me, the project of WGST has always been the work of imagining and building a more inclusive, equitable, and just future. Both educators and students will find in "Why WGST?" not only new knowledge and skills but also—to quote the poet and feminist activist, Adrienne Rich (2003) "a new, expanded sense of what's humanly possible" (p. 26)."

---

### Teaching Concept Overview—Why WGST?

**Purpose:** These opening units introduce core WGST concepts and connect those to justice work locally and globally. In addition to broadly overviewing many feminisms and concepts, scholars also engage in research around the United Nations fifth Sustainable Development Goal (SDG) and map these targets to advocacy work in their local communities. Finally, scholars consider their own lived experiences, identities, and perceptions of feminisms and gender. This is deeply reflective work on which your class communities can continue to build throughout subsequent units.

### ✔ Objectives

By the end of these units, scholars will be able to:

- ◆ Connect the United Nations' SDG 5 to local advocacy work.
- ◆ Define many types of feminisms and start to identify theories and methodologies they resonate with.
- ◆ Explain some of the nuances of gender as a social construct and name specific ways groups and individuals have expanded our understanding of gender.
- ◆ Analyze texts by feminist scholars including bell hooks, Sojourner Truth, Emma Watson, and Chimamanda Adichie.
- ◆ Interview an elder on gender advocacy.

? **Essential Questions for Scholars**

- ◆ What can I learn about gender justice from transnational and global perspectives?
- ◆ How does the way gender is socially constructed affect my peers and me?
- ◆ What does feminism and justice mean to me?

(II) **Reflective Questions for Educators**

- ◆ What justice issues (local and global) are centered in my curriculum?
- ◆ How can I advance greater gender, racial, ethnic, and linguistic representation in my curricular choices?
- ◆ How can my teaching contribute to further global awareness and student-led projects related to equity and justice?

| Activate Prior Knowledge—Feminist T-Shirts | |
|---|---|
| **Unit 1—Feminist Theory: Introduction** | **Unit 2—We Can All Be Changemakers for Justice** |
| Lesson 1—United Nations' SDG 5: Exploration<br>Lesson 2—What is WGST?<br>Lesson 3—"Two Spirit:" Gender as a Social Construct | Lesson 1—Ain't I A Woman?: Sojourner Truth<br>Lesson 2—If Not You, Who? Sowing the Seeds of Advocacy<br>Lesson 3—Feminisms Are for Everybody: bell hooks |
| Synthesis Project—WGST & Me | |

## Concept 1—Dedications

**Kathryn's Dedication**—I dedicate this section to a young person we'll call Mae.[1] A month or so into her ninth-grade year, Mae asked me if she could talk to me about something. We found a quiet corner in the counselor's office. She said she had been reading about mental health in the LGBTQIA+ community. Over the next four years, she would continue to bring pertinent research to our classroom so that we could learn together. Mae said she knew it was important to identify safe and caring adults with whom she could be fully herself. She then told me that she is nonbinary and uses the pronouns she/them.

What they said next is one of the most important things a student has ever said to me. "If I only talk to one person about my identity this year, I think it should be you."

With hope, Mae's words will always stick with me. I chose them for my chapter dedication because their message speaks to how much teachers matter. I also chose them because Mae actively asked for more WGST coursework in their high school experience. They helped organize a research study on feminism at our high school and presented that work to graduate students at a university symposium. In short, Mae believed in this project before Jill and I had even dreamt it up.

While working with Jill on these lessons, I thought of Mae and several other bright young people who have participated in student-led advocacy projects with me over the years. I didn't think of Mae as she is now, a vibrant professional, confident, and successful in her various endeavors, but as she was in her teenage years, when she was seeking more representative lessons in her classes and more inclusive practices in our school. We (Kathryn and Jill) want to deliver on that wish and want to do so with tools, strategies, and vocabulary to support you in teaching toward a more inclusive world.

**Jill's Dedication**—I would like to dedicate this section to my daughter, Amélie. As I write this dedication, Amélie is a first-year student at the University of Missouri, Kansas City. Along with being a student, she is working, living on her own, and managing it all with a mix of tangled anxiety and beautiful confidence. Just as my heart feels a bit splintered since she has left home, it also brims with pride at who she has become and who she is becoming.

In this book, we (Jill and Kathryn) often reference those upon whose shoulders we stand in this important, expansive work of gender equity. Often, this refers to the shoulders of our ancestors, and while I, too, stand on the shoulders of those who have gone before me, I stand, at least as much, upon my daughter's shoulders. As I work with Kathryn on the lessons in this book, I so often think of Amélie and am inspired by her. She is full of wisdom, empathy, kindness, passion, and strength. She is an advocate for gender equity and intersectional justice and is a champion of inclusion. She is living a story of courage and compassion, and her story invites me to live my own story, as an educator and a human, with courage and compassion, as well.

When I think of the scholars that these two units will reach, I think of my daughter. I want to write lessons that she would have loved as a high school student. I want to write lessons that would have resonated with her own story. I want to write lessons that would have expanded the ideas of the other scholars in her school. I want to write lessons that could have bolstered her courage and confidence.

When I think of the scholars that these two units will reach, I also think of **you**. It was Amélie's middle school and high school teachers who truly helped her settle into who she is and who inspired within her the courage to live her own story. They loved her, encouraged her, gave her a safe space to retreat to, and filled their snack drawers with her favorite flavor of Pop-Tarts. We (Kathryn and I) hope to share tools and strategies with you as you help students live out their stories of courage and compassion, justice, and inclusion. This section introducing WGST to your scholars will hopefully lay a foundation for those stories to be both told and lived.

## Concept Introduction by Kathryn and Jill

You are a vibrant constellation of identities, experiences, and cultures. You may be living out the boldest dreams of your ancestors. And you are here, engaging in teaching and learning about WGST. Like us (Kathryn and Jill), you likely believe that this work matters, that young people matter, that together we can co-create a more just world. Across the following units, you will remind scholars that they, too, are a vibrant constellation of identities, experiences, and cultures. They are the boldest dreams of their ancestors. They are here and can be leaders in co-creating a more just world.

We (Kathryn and Jill) believe that WGST calls us to:

◆ think critically across disciplines and points of view;
◆ offer and celebrate more complete stories of history, culture, and identity;
◆ affirm a multiplicity of lived experiences and perspectives; and
◆ work to further the cause of justice and equity while also reducing oppression and marginalization.

This is a lofty work in what is already a high-stakes profession. As educators ourselves, we know that teaching is heart- and head-heavy work. It asks so much of both teacher and learner—terms that are often interchangeable. For this reason, please see our letters of care and support at the start of each new teaching concept. We (Kathryn and Jill) hope these letters offer you some encouragement for the noble task of teaching for a more just world, tips for navigating the unit content, and an invitation to make choices for the best interest of you and your scholars' well-being.

The following two units introduce core concepts from this book including justice, feminism, representation, gender, inclusion, identity, and equity. They ask scholars to begin to consider their own lived experiences, identities, and perceptions. This process might be uncomfortable for some scholars, as their concepts of gender and feminism may be challenged. Other scholars may find in these lessons an expression of beliefs they could not quite articulate before or an outlet for passions they did not know how to pursue. In these units, our hope is for scholars to have the space for growth, reflection, questioning, stretching, and transformation. In these stage-setting units, scholars are introduced to the tension between celebrating a multiplicity of stories and recognizing a specific pattern of gendered experiences and discrimination. Throughout the book, scholars (and educators) may want to return to these early reflections, questions, and impressions to track change and personal growth.

## Educator Letter for Concept 1—*It Should be You*

Dear Valued Educator,

These letters are our gift to you. They are a connecting space for us (Kathryn and Jill) to share some moments thinking together about the chapter content and what care might look like **for you** in teaching these big important ideas. We hope these letters (1) offer grounding information about why this work, *your work in the classroom,* matters and (2) give you specific ideas for care strategies as you embark on this important work.

**Your Work Matters**

If these lessons stir up something important in your scholars, as we (Kathryn and Jill) hope they do, you may be that one adult a young person identifies as their safe person. The Trevor Project's 2020 National Survey on LGBTQ Youth Mental Health (The Trevor Project, n.d.) reports that these relationships, classroom conversations, and culture of support can literally save lives. They also report that this is urgent work.

- ◆ Forty percent of LGBTQ respondents seriously considered attempting suicide in the past 12 months, with more than half of transgender and nonbinary youth having seriously considered suicide.
- ◆ Sixty-eight percent of LGBTQ youth reported symptoms of generalized anxiety disorder in the past two weeks, including more than three in four transgender and nonbinary youth.
- ◆ Forty-six percent of LGBTQ youth report they wanted psychological or emotional counseling from a mental health professional but were unable to receive it in the past 12 months.

These statistics from the Trevor Project are an updated version of the research Mae (p. 13) brought me several years ago. Mae read a report like this, wasn't sure what to do with it, and then brought it to a trusted teacher.

We suspect that you, too, will have scholar conversations that begin, "Can I tell you something?" and end with equal parts weight and light in your heart. These conversations can happen with any of your scholars. Every scholar in your classroom is navigating unique and complicated experiences. Teaching WGST is deeply personal work and as such it often leads to scholars giving you their weights and hopes. Because of this, we want to encourage you right here at the onset of these units to set up a care plan—for yourself.

**Care Strategies for Educators**

◆ **Who are the colleague allies that you can go to for problem solving and support?** Identity those folks now, and if possible, include someone from your school's mental health team on your list. You may also want to identify a partner teacher that you can co-teach some of these lessons with.

◆ **What does self-care mean for you?** Does it look like a quiet walk in the morning, a yoga class on Thursdays, or cooking a favorite meal? Name several things that bring you joy and calm and put two on your calendar for this week and every week that follows.

◆ **Why are you teaching WGST?** Spend some time reflecting on this question early in your class studies. Your answer may surprise you, inspire you, and even guide your teaching.

Thank you for engaging in this noble work. If we only reach one educator with this book, we think it should be you.

With admiration,

Kathryn and Jill

## Activate Prior Knowledge—Feminist T-Shirts

**Teaching Notes**

The activity we use to activate prior knowledge requires honesty, courage, and ample reflective space. In this activity, scholars respond to three statements, reflect individually, and then share their ideas in a whole-class dialogue. Scholars are asked to defend (agree), refute (disagree), or qualify (clarify or revise) each of the statements. Regardless of the position they choose, scholars are also asked to justify this position. This structure invites critical thinking and multiple answers and honors the wide range of perspectives in your class.

Before holding the dialogue, remind scholars of any class the ground rules or norms you use in your work together, such as assuming positive intent, recognizing that all experiences are valid, practicing courage, and monitoring patterns of participation. Norms that reinforce that all voices and experiences have value in this conversation are essential to an inclusive politics in your classroom and feminist discourse around these ideas. Some of your scholars may have a background in feminisms and already be engaged in justice work. These experiences are important in this conversation. However, so, too, are the experiences of scholars who have not yet had access to feminism scholarship, had to think deeply about gender before, or who do not yet see themselves as leaders and changemakers (recognizing that there may be many reasons for this). As an educator, you can invite and affirm a multiplicity of voices in each of these lessons.

After scholars have had the opportunity to reflect individually, facilitate a class wide dialogue on these statements. Remind scholars there is no *right answer* to these questions. All of the perspectives and experiences that scholars bring to our class and to this activity can help deepen our collective learning. Invite scholars to share their justifications. On the surface, most people (though not all) agree with most of the content in the initial three statements. However, as we peel back the layers and share questions, quandaries, and corrections, this conversation becomes more critical and more complex. For example, statement 1, "Girls and women should have access to the same opportunities as boys and men," is an opportunity to ask how trans and nonbinary people are included (or excluded) in this statement.

Following this opener, scholars will then design their own feminist t-shirts. These shirts offer a creative way for scholars to share what feminism and justice mean to them. There should be as many different t-shirt designs as there are scholars in your class. How each student identifies and the experiences each student brings to your class matter. As scholars share their designs, remind them that in this space, we honor that all experiences are valid. As you dive into this content, create space to acknowledge assumptions, complicated feelings, questions, and biases you and your classes have around the term: *feminism*. You may personally find you have some of these beliefs and discomfort even if you fundamentally believe in affirming the rights and opportunities of all genders.

Over the next two units, your class will connect these statements to both the United Nations' SDG 5 and feminist movements. This may lead to some big questions about gender, bias, equity, and justice.

As our class community begins to engage with these lessons on WGST, take a moment to analyze the beliefs you hold about empowerment, opportunity, and equity. To start this conversation, read and consider each statement below. These statements are informed by the United Nations' SDG 5.

| Term | Definition |
|---|---|
| United Nations' Sustainable Development Goals (SDGs) | The United Nations' Sustainable Development plan outlines 17 goals called the SDGs for peace, prosperity, and wellbeing for humanity and the planet we share. While gender threads across all SDGs, SDG 5 focuses directly on gender equality and empowerment. |

Mark whether you would defend (agree), refute (disagree) or qualify (clarify/revise) these three statements. Then write your justifications (rationale) for your decisions. Some of these statements may bring up big feelings or questions for you. If so, note those and any reflections, as well.

| | Statement | Defend, Refute, Qualify | Reflection and Justification |
|---|---|---|---|
| 1 | Girls and women should have access to the same opportunities as boys and men. | | ✎ |
| 2 | It is important to work for the social, economic, and political equality of the sexes. | | ✎ |
| 3 | All people (including children) should live in a world where they feel safe in their homes, neighborhoods, and communities. | | ✎ |

These three statements guide the work of the United Nations' Sustainable Development Goal #5, which is to *Achieve gender equality and empower all women and girls* (United Nations, n.d.-c). They also are core feminist beliefs.

## Feminist T-Shirts

One of my (Kathryn's) alumna scholars, whom we'll call Jasmyn, was home from college during her winter break. She stopped by to see me and we visited over coffee. I asked about her science classes, extracurriculars, and the latest books she was reading. She answered and then sharply turned our conversation to feminism. Jasmyn was frustrated with a lack of depth in the ways her peers talked about and practiced feminism.

> I mean, everyone gets a feminist t-shirt before the semester starts. Obviously, I can't imagine anyone at my school saying that they weren't a feminist, but you know most people aren't really *doing* anything about feminism. Like, if you're going to get a t-shirt that says you're a feminist, shouldn't you be working toward racial justice, inclusion for LGBTQIA+ students on campus, or volunteering at your local health clinic to help address health disparities?

Jasmyn was engaging in all of these actions and more; however, if I were to mention that, she would be quick to turn the focus away from herself.

"Look," I can almost hear her saying, "If you are doing the work, you don't need a shirt, and if you aren't doing the work, the shirt doesn't mean anything."

I wasn't familiar with the feminist t-shirt events that Jasmyn kept mentioning, so I asked her about this. She told me that a couple days before fall semester each year, there is a big event on her school quad. The event includes live music, signups for student activities, and feminist t-shirts. She told me:

> Everyone gets one. They come in a variety of sayings, you know, like, *As strong as the woman next to me; feminism is the radical notion that women are people;* and *this is what a feminist looks like.* They're all great messages. I just want it to mean something to the wearer.

Jasmyn thought the t-shirts themselves were fine but only if they translated to action. This begs an interesting question to consider. *What would your feminist t-shirt say?* What is a value, commitment, or challenge you feel so strongly about that you would not only wear it on your person but also put it into action in the choices you make in your community? You do not have to choose one of the phrases listed above or any other phrase you have seen on a t-shirt. Be authentic to your core values. Take a moment to design your own feminist shirt and then share with a peer why you chose that message, quote, or phrase.

You might use these questions to process together:

- What did you think about while drawing?
- What does your feminist t-shirt say about what you believe and value?
- To borrow from Jasmyn's wisdom, how will you make this shirt *mean something*?
- If we could print these shirts tomorrow, would you wear them? Why or why not?

**Closer.** To close this activity, review the first three statements, reflect on our conversation in class today, and then respond to these last two statements using our same protocol from the start of class.

| | Statement | Defend, Refute, Qualify | Reflection and Justification |
|---|---|---|---|
| 4 | The United Nations' Sustainable Development Goal 5—*to achieve gender equality and empower all girls and women*—is an important and worthwhile goal. | | ✎ |
| 5 | Feminism is for everybody. | | ✎ |

# Unit 1—Feminist Theory: Introduction

As our early lessons and experiences in both the classroom and the world suggest, there is a lot of confusion about what feminism means, who feminism is for, and how these ideals might function in our communities and change movements. Throughout this book, we study feminist scholars and activists and their work around race, gender, identity, access, voice, and advocacy. These big concepts are often grounded in the everyday context of our lived experiences. In this text, we define feminism as *an affirmation of humanity that seeks freedom from oppression and commits to the full access of social, economic, and political rights and opportunities for all people.* Throughout these lessons, scholars will learn more about multiple feminist frameworks and feminisms including radical feminisms, Black feminisms, queer theory, and transnational and global feminisms. As they do, scholars and educators will be able to build a feminist politic grounded in their own lived experiences, unique views, and commitments.

In this opening unit, scholars consider the multiplicity of identities, stories, and experiences that contribute to specific patterns related to discrimination, access, representation, and safety. This unit introduces core concepts including justice, feminism, gender, inclusion, and equity. As we consider the global scale of feminist work, scholars explore the United Nations' SDG 5 on gender equality and empowerment seeking to better understand how human rights and opportunities are affirmed or denied. In addition to looking out at global issues, scholars also look in to examine their own lived experiences, identities, and perceptions of feminism and gender.

We (Kathryn and Jill) don't expect or require that all scholars identify as feminists. We do, however, aim to create contexts where scholars are inspired to work toward equity and justice, where they bring forward critical challenges related to inclusion and representation, and where they feel empowered to lead actions focused on ending injustice and oppression.

---

**Key Term: *Lived Experiences***

Have you heard the phrase *no one does you better than you*? An extension of this phrase may be *no one knows you and your experiences better than you*. Lived experiences are the primary source account of the experiences, choices, everyday activities, and knowledge a person has gained through their direct involvement with the world.

Focusing on lived experiences emphasizes that you are the most qualified person to report on your lives and experiences. Further, your experiences are a source of knowledge. In 1970, Carol Hanisch published an article titled "The personal is political." This deep-seated belief that our lived experiences hold knowledge and map against collective trends, including structural oppression and challenges, is a cornerstone of many of the feminist theories we study in the following lessons.

These lessons emphasize that all experiences are valid, that people are experts on their own lives, and that personal stories have the power to build bridges and increase understanding.

### Related Term: *Intersectionality*

Intersectionality is a framework for understanding how multiple identities and *systems of oppressions* intersect to create specific experiences and conditions within systems. These experiences include systems of advantage (power and privilege) and disadvantage (discrimination and oppression). For example, these may include the compounding effects of racism and sexism or racism and heterosexism or racism, sexism, and heterosexism. This framework centers the experiences and "voices of those experiencing overlapping, concurrent forms of oppression in order to understand the depths of the inequalities and the relationships among them in any given context" (UN Women, 2020, para 5). Recognizing the first-person experiences and stories of individuals from historically marginalized and multiply marginalized backgrounds as important sites for knowledge is inherent to intersectional approaches. (See also descriptions of *Black feminisms* and *Kimberlé Crenshaw's* work that we explore throughout this book.)

### Related Term: *Asset-Based Approaches*

Asset-based approaches, also called s*trengths-based approaches,* seek to recognize and leverage the unique skills, talents, and strengths of individuals and communities. These approaches acknowledge that while systems or institutions may be broken or in need of repair, people bring genius, talents, and inherent worth to our communities.

### Teaching Notes

Mature Content—Sexual Violence

Over the next two lessons, scholars will explore the United Nations' SDG 5 targets which include some difficult content around violence and sexual violence. We (Kathryn and Jill) know that different school communities and grade bands will have different guidelines about addressing this content in class. We also know that this topic may be personally triggering to individual scholars and educators.

To keep this lesson as accessible as possible, we did not include some of the more difficult language around female genital mutilation in our lesson materials; however, scholars may find this in their own research. With younger scholars (Grades 9–10), you may want to point them to specific, vetted resources that are appropriate for your class community. Likewise, in the Adichie speech, "We Should All be Feminists," there is a reference to a gang rape. The reference is brief and you could fast forward through it without missing the speaker's overall meaning.

*As always, you are best able to make decisions about what content is appropriate for the scholars in your classes.*

For those who do choose to teach about how sexual violence, violence against women, and female genital mutilation fit within the United Nations' Sustainable Development Goals, we encourage you to proceed with caution and humanity. Below are four important reminders for this work.

◆ Avoid any victim-blaming language. The perpetrators of gender-based violence against women are to blame for violence against women. Full stop.

◆ Guard against ethnocentrism or us/them language. Violence against women is not something that happens "in other places." It is a danger we all live with in every community.

◆ Scholars may have anatomical questions related to this content. I (Kathryn) find it helpful to lean on my peers in health and science education for these conversations. When I taught in public high schools, I frequently invited supportive biology and anatomy teachers to my classroom to field scholars' questions and help me facilitate the scientific parts of these conversations.

◆ Finally, remember that educators do not know all of the lived experiences of their scholars. Be upfront about the topics you will cover before diving into the content. Give scholars permission to take care of themselves, to take a break, and to go speak with a counselor. Remind scholars that you also are a safe person to process with if they need to share something difficult that this lesson may have brought up. Also give yourself permission to take care of yourself including seeking support for any feelings this content may stir up in you.

**Mandated Reporting**—Many of you are also *mandated reporters*. This means when and if young people bring you experiences of abuse, neglect, or immediate danger, there is a system of reporting that you are legally required to put in place. To support you in the moment of these difficult situations, here is a modified script I (Kathryn) have used in my work with young people in these cases:

> Oh, [NAME]. That took so much courage to share. Thank you for trusting me with this difficult story. I also need you to know that because this experience is affecting your safety, we will have to bring another person into this conversation. I will be right here with you the whole time. Do you have an administrator or counselor that you trust? If so, let me know, and I'll arrange that conversation. In the meantime, you can stay right here with me. [NAME], I care about you and want to keep you safe.

While the young person can't decide whether or not you report the information, you can still look for opportunities for agency and commit to care and transparency throughout the process.

Navigating the responsibility and pain of hotlining an abuse incident is challenging for educators, too. It is also not something you have to do on your own. You can report with a counselor or administrator. Many districts have an "employee assistance program" that covers confidential therapy support for educators. A mentor of mine recently shared that he recommends scheduling a therapy conversation for yourself anytime you have to report abuse. I (Kathryn) think this is brilliant advice. By taking care of your own mental health, you are more able to take care of the mental health of your students.

## Lesson 1: United Nations' SDG 5—Exploration

 **Thought Questions**

◆ What makes an issue a local issue?
◆ What makes an issue a global issue?
◆ For example, is food insecurity a local issue or a global issue?
◆ What about gender-based discrimination?

These issues, like all issues we will explore in these lessons, are complex. They are both global and local. Engaging in justice work requires us to look deeply at both how issues map across contexts and what this means in local contexts, including our own schools and communities.

In this opening lesson, you will explore gender-related issues that the United Nations (UN) has named important for our global community. Before diving into these issues, we want to introduce three key terms: *global feminisms, transnational feminism,*[2] and the *United Nations' Sustainable Development Goals (SDGs)*.

| Term | Definition |
|---|---|
| **Global feminisms** | The intentional study of feminisms from around the world. This study is grounded in an ethics of inclusion. Global feminisms explore local feminisms and justice movements, transnational approaches (or those that move beyond geographical boundaries), and global trends such as those in the United Nations' SDGs. The Vanderbilt Global Feminisms Collaborative (n.d.) writes:<br><br>Global feminisms scholars are engaged in the study of boundaries associated with sex, gender, sexuality, class, race, ability, ethnicity, geography, identity, and membership—using both theoretical and empirical lenses. They are attentive to silence and marginalization, to citizenship politics |

| Term | Definition |
|---|---|
| | (including migration, refugees, rights, and participation), to political economy (formal and informal), to society and culture, and to the environment (understood as the places where we live, work, play, and pray).<br><br>(para 3) |
| **Transnational feminisms** | A methodology that seeks global action and understanding. It strives to move beyond individual nations or nation-states to engage in a more collective production of knowledge. |

As you explore feminist frameworks throughout the following lessons, think critically about the claims being made and the context in which they are made. See if you can identify inherent blind spots or biases in how information is presented. Everyone has blind spots and biases. One of the objectives of these WGST lessons is to help you see these more clearly so that you can fill gaps in understanding and work to reduce your own biases. Critiques matter—they push each of us toward that next best version. And yet, you can also spend too much time in criticism. After a certain period of wrestling with a new idea, a grounding question to come back to is this: *How can I use this idea to further the cause of justice?*

"Rather than asking what transnational feminism *is*," Asha Nadkarni and Subhalakshmi Gooptu (2017) write, "it is more useful to think about what transnational feminist theorizing *does* or makes possible" (para 1). As you explore the United Nations' Sustainable Development Goals, focus on solutions, actions, and advocacy. Recognizing that these issues are both local and global, pay attention to context, nuance, and the different realities of the various communities you are exploring, including your own local and school communities.

Name _____ Date _____

**Directions:** Working in teams, select one of the focus priorities below and create a six-slide presentation for your peers. Your slides should address the following:

◆ What area of gender justice is your team focused on?
◆ What United Nations targets does this relate to? Define any key terms that might be unfamiliar to your peers.
◆ Name one important global trend related to this issue.
◆ Identify a local (school or city) connection to this issue and an organization or person who is working for positive change.
◆ How could you and your peers support this work?
◆ Cite your sources.

Later, you will have the opportunity to learn with classmates who researched a different priority. You can use the chart below to take notes during your peers' presentations.

## Exploring United Nations' Sustainable Development Goal 5
### *Achieve gender equality and empower all women and girls.*

| Key Point | Topics | United Nations Targets | Notes |
|---|---|---|---|
| Expand equality and end discrimination. | Nondiscrimination, voting, legislation, and empowerment | End discrimination against women and girls (5.1). Adopt and strengthen policies and enforceable legislation for gender equality (5.C). | |
| Expand reproductive health and end violence. | Physical and psychological safety, reproductive health care, education | End all violence and exploitation against women and girls (5.2). Eliminate forced and child marriages (5.3). Universal access to reproductive rights and health (5.6). | |
| Create equal leadership and economic opportunities. | Politics, decision making, leadership, property | Ensure full participation in leadership and decision-making (5.5). Equal rights to economic resources, property ownership and financial services (5.A). | |
| Expand mobility and value domestic work. | Mobile telephone ownership, household, family | Promote empowerment of women through technology (5.B). Value unpaid care and promote shared domestic responsibilities (5.4). | |

*Sources: United Nations, SDG Tracker; United Nations' SDG 5*

**Teaching Notes**

This lesson introduces scholars to a definition of both WGST and feminism. In this text, we (Jill and Kathryn) define feminism as *an affirmation of humanity that seeks freedom from oppression and commits to the full access of social, economic, and political rights and opportunities for all people*. This is a layered definition! Scholars have already begun thinking about what feminism is by exploring SDG 5 and creating their own feminist t-shirts. Now, they will work collaboratively to break down this definition of feminism into its component parts and analyze what each part means to them and to their peers. As with the SDG activity, remind scholars that there is not a singular "right way" to fill in this chart. In fact, the multiplicity of perspectives and experiences that each scholar brings to the dialogue creates a rich space for exploration, thought, and discussion.

You could create a large anchor chart with this definition and have scholars populate the chart with Post-it notes. This can also work online, as well. When we (Kathryn and Jill) facilitated this activity with a group of educators, we shared a Google Doc of this chart, and educators spent a few moments populating the chart with their ideas about how to unpack each component of the definition. Then, we talked through this brainstorm together.

This chart can serve as an important and living reference as you and your scholars explore these lessons. Having it accessible throughout the units may serve as a helpful teaching tool.

## Lesson 2: What Is WGST?

Name _____ Date_____

> **Women's and Gender Studies (WGST)**—An interdisciplinary study of the ways gender is constructed and how it affects our lived experiences and opportunities; a commitment to work toward greater justice and equity; and the intentional centering of stories, histories, and contributions of women and girls that are too often missing from curricula and media.

---

 **Thought Questions**

◆ In reading this definition of WGST, what surprises or interests you?

---

WGST spans the arts, humanities, social sciences, and sciences. Throughout the lessons in this book, we focus on three main aspects of WGST.

◆ **Analysis**—How is gender constructed, and in what ways do these beliefs affect our lived experiences and opportunities?
◆ **Advocacy**—How can we work toward greater justice, equality, and equity?
◆ **Representation**—In what areas do we need to work toward greater gender representation? How can we center and celebrate more contributions, stories, and histories?

### Activating Prior Knowledge—Women's and Gender Studies

You and your peers bring important knowledge, experiences, and background to these themes. On the following page is a chart to fill out in small groups.

# *Start Where You Are*—Feminism

Name _____ Date_____

Scholar Chart—Let's break down this definition into its components. What does each part mean to you and your peers?[3]

| Feminism: An affirmation of humanity that seeks freedom from oppression and commits to the full access of social, health, economic, and political rights and opportunities for all people. | | | | | |
|---|---|---|---|---|---|
| *Affirmation of humanity* | *Freedom from oppression* | *Social rights and opportunities* | *Health rights and opportunities* | *Economic rights and opportunities* | *Political rights and opportunities* | *For all people* |
| | | | | | | |

*Equity* and *equality* are two terms you will come across throughout this book, and while they may sound similar, they are actually quite different. While some feminist movements, including liberal feminisms, have fought for equality of rights and opportunities, others, such as radical feminisms and Black feminisms, have fought for equity.

Equality means everyone receives the same regardless of need. For example, let's imagine that a school principal recently learned that two of her eigth graders were having a hard time reading the fine print in their English literature text. In response, she wrote a grant for free reading glasses for all eighth graders at her school. This kind of equality approach sounds great—free reading glasses for everyone, and it might help the two students who were having a hard time with the text, as well as others who are slightly nearsighted. However, the reading glasses would offer insufficient correction for people who are farsighted or visually impaired, and they would be a nuisance to people with very strong vision. Further, if young people have other obstacles to literacy education, including learning disabilities, the reading glasses wouldn't help and would be considered a waste of resources. This isn't to say that all approaches grounded in equality are problematic; some have been very important. For example, in my (Kathryn's) local school district, administrators now give *all* scholars and families information about accessing free and reduced-price lunches. This is a change from when families used to have to opt in to receive the information or counselors had to reach out to specific individuals they thought might benefit from the information. By making the same information available to all, the school district is able to better support families who may be moving in and out of food insecurity.

Equity, on the other hand, looks deeply at systems to determine needs and root causes of injustice to consider how local and individual context affects challenges and solutions. An equity approach to this same challenge with the two eighth graders might be to survey the grade 8 class to learn who else is struggling with the text and who is excelling. It might involve getting reading glasses or a large print version for the initial two scholars, but it may also reveal that there is a small group of recent immigrants who need more language intervention. Rather than using resources to give everyone the same resource (e.g. reading glasses), this approach seeks to look deeply at systems, identify specific needs, and respond to those contextualized needs so that everyone has an opportunity to thrive. In the free-and-reduced lunch example, an equity approach might go even further to consider additional wrap-around services such as access to food banks, pantries, and weekend snack packs, as well as health and economic supports related to hunger.

During your studies, you will encounter many new vocabulary terms like these. Below are five key concepts we have started exploring in these early WGST lessons.

| Term | Definition |
|---|---|
| Equality | Having the same status, rights, and opportunities. |
| Equity | Fairness and justice; equity is different from equality (see above) in that it recognizes that different people have different experiences, opportunities, access, and needs. Because of this, equity work requires systematic change to remove barriers, adjust imbalances, and create more just solutions and systems. |
| Feminism | Freedom from oppression, an affirmation of humanity, and a commitment to the full access of social, economic, health, and political rights and opportunities for all people. (See also the definitions and discussion of Black feminisms, transnational and global feminisms, queer theory, liberal feminisms, and radical feminisms.) |
| Gender | Socially constructed and culturally specific roles, behaviors, and identities of being feminine, masculine, or a combination of traits |
| Sex | A label (female or male) assigned at birth based on reproductive anatomy, chromosomes, and biology |
| Scholarship | The academic study of and/or commitment to learning at a high level. |

## Vocabulary Connections

Reflect on your SDG 5 research presentations. Connect some of these vocabulary words to your research on that activity.

| Term | Reflection Question |
|---|---|
| Equality | How does *equality* affect the issues or solutions you explored? |
| Equity | How does *equity* affect the issues or solutions you explored? |
| Equality vs. equity | Do you believe it is more important to work for equality or equity on this issue? Defend your answer with specific examples. |
| Feminism and justice | How is justice, including social or racial justice, embedded in the issue you studied? |
| Scholarship | How is *scholarship* important in advancing work on this issue? Offer specific examples. |

## Lesson 3: "Two Spirit"—Gender as a Social Construct

**Teaching Note**

This unit introduces the idea that gender is a social construct. This concept is typically new for high school scholars and can lead to important conversations about the differences between sex (biology) and gender (culture). The lesson is divided into four distinct parts. Depending on the conversation following each section, you may find you need an extra class period or two to work through this content together.

◆ First, scholars are briefly introduced to ideas about the ways gender is socially constructed. This introduction invites scholars to imagine new possibilities and to celebrate a multiplicity of identities.

◆ Next is a short dialogue that builds on gender as a social construct. This dialogue is written in a more casual tone to invite scholars to ask similar candid questions as they explore these new concepts.

◆ Third, scholars review lesson vocabulary related to gender-expansive identities. If you have a GSA (gay-straight alliance) or other similar student group, you might invite the faculty sponsor to help you facilitate questions and clarifications about these terms.

◆ The lesson ends with readings on gender identities beyond the binary including two-spirit traditions in Native American Indigenous communities, *the kathoey* in Thailand, and *the hijra* in India. Depending on your class, you may want to read these aloud to everyone so that you can respond together and so that you are available to help with questions. We have also provided a PCR (prior knowledge-connections-research) chart to accompany this lesson and help scholars organize their notes. Throughout these readings, scholars consider how colonization has oppressed and restricted gender expression and more expansive identities. This last section offers the possibility for strong social studies connections on the harm and destruction caused by colonization, violence, and settler politics across Indigenous communities worldwide.

Simone de Beauvoir famously said, "One is not born, but rather becomes a woman." In this quote, de Beauvoir is referring to the difference between sex and gender, namely that gender is constantly being negotiated and constructed. Judith Butler (1956–), an American philosopher and gender theorist, whose book *Gender Trouble* (1990 followed by a second edition in 1999) remains a seminal queer theory text, writes that these categories and identities related to gender have the potential to be unmade and remade; however, because they are rooted in systems of power, acts of resistance carry risk.

These lessons invite you to imagine and celebrate new possibilities. Joy can be a form of resistance. Pride, also, be an act of resistance. In this lesson, you will read about the bright expansiveness of gender and gender identity. This bright expansiveness holds true across time, geography, and culture. Gender and the ways an individual expresses their gender identity may be in concert or conflict with the cultural norms of specific communities and historical periods. These tensions between expectations, social constructs, and the vast range of experiences may reinforce ideas about gender, reject ideas about gender, or introduce new ideas about what it means to be human.

**Gender Is a Social Construct—A Dialogue**

Scholar 1: Today we learned about the ways gender is socially constructed.

Scholar 2: What does that even mean? Are you saying that gender isn't real because gender feels pretty real to me?

Scholar 2: Sure. Our social constructs give us real information. They guide our behavior, inform identity, and are often reinforced in dangerous ways. When social theorists say that gender is a social construct, they aren't saying that it isn't real. They are simply saying it isn't biologically determined or static. What gender means changes across time, culture, situation, and person.

Scholar 2: Woah. Ummm. Not biologically determined? There are some biological differences between guys and gals.

Scholar 1: Sure, there are some biological differences between the sexes (female, male, intersex, etc). However, sex and gender aren't the same thing.

Scholar 2: Intersex?

Scholar 1: Yep, lots of people are born with a reproductive anatomy that doesn't fit our limited binary definitions of female or male.

Scholar 2: Lots of people?

Scholar 1: We read a 2021 article by Amnesty International, which reported that about 1.7% of babies born are intersex. This is about the same number of babies born with red hair.

Scholar 2: Well, if it's so common, why didn't I know about it before?

Scholar 1: Once a social construct is created, it has to be socially reinforced er to gain meaning. If, for example, part of our social construct for gender in the United States is that there are only two options, then individuals with genders, identities, or anatomical parts outside of this binary are often forced to the margins. Social constructs lose their power through non-examples.

Scholar 1: Oh. I see it. The same is probably true for my trans friends, huh?

Scholar 2: For sure. However, these constructs don't only limit the LGBTQIA+ community. They limit all of us. This is how we get a culture that teaches boys not to cry even when they are sad and girls not to be too loud even when they feel something strongly.

Scholar: Yeah. . . .

| Term | Definition |
|---|---|
| Social construct | An idea that has been created, accepted, and reinforced across a cultural group (e.g. gender and race) |
| Cisgender | People whose gender aligns with the sex they were assigned at birth. For example, if a baby was assigned male at birth and identifies as a boy/man, he would be considered cisgender (or cis). |
| Transgender | People whose gender does not align with the sex they were assigned at birth. For example, if a baby was assigned male at birth and later identifies as a girl/woman, she may be transgender (or trans). |
| Intersex | A general term used for a variety of situations in which a person's reproductive anatomy doesn't fit the binary definitions of "female" or "male." |
| Gender-expansive | An umbrella term for people whose gender expression and identity are beyond or outside a specific gender identity, category, or label. As an umbrella term, *gender-expansive* encompasses many different identities. Some gender-expansive people use this term when referencing their gender identity, and some prefer other related terms. For example, <br><br> ◆ Some gender-expansive people identify with a spectrum of genders and may use the term *nonbinary*. <br> ◆ Some gender-expansive people identify primarily with a single gender and may use the term *transgender*, <br> ◆ And still other gender-expansive people may identify without a gender and use the term *agender*. <br><br> As with all identity labels, it is important to honor the terms and language individuals identify with while also respecting that language can change over time. |

Because gender is a social construct, it is also culturally specific. The roles, behaviors, and identities considered appropriate for specific genders vary across cultures and over time. As we continue in our learning, we will explore some of these cultural differences in our study of *the kathoey* from Thailand, *"two-spirit"* people in the Navajo nations; *the hijra* in India; and trans, non-binary, gender nonconforming, and gender-expansive identities in our own communities and beyond.

**Beyond the Binary: Lesson Notes (PCR)**

Name_____ Date_____

| | PRIOR KNOWLEDGE<br>*What You Already Know* | CURIOSITIES<br>*What You Want to Know* | RESEARCH<br>*Questions and Sources to Explore* |
|---|---|---|---|
| Colonization | | | |
| Gender-expansive identities | | | |
| Thailand<br>India<br>Native cultures in the United States | | | |

| Term | Definition |
|------|------------|
| Colonization | To violently establish control over the Indigenous people of an area. This control is intended to benefit those coming to the land and colonizing, even at the great harm of those who have previously cared for and called the land home. In addition to physical harm, Indigenous traditions and culture are often devalued or destroyed during colonization. |
| Binary | Consisting of only two parts. |

Many cultures have long recognized, revered, and celebrated more than two genders. In the next section, you will learn about gender identities that transcend binary definitions. These are just a few examples among many. Before beginning these readings, it is important to emphasize that gender and identity are vast. Further, this vastness is even more complex when considered across our global community (Pattanaik, 2019). The following short readings are *brief summaries,* meaning they offer a starting place and are also incomplete. Further, because these stories transcend culture and language, some of the terms and interpretations have been translated from their original context several times.[4] As you explore these examples, read with an open mind and heart, recognizing that your own experiences, culture, and language influence your worldview and your approach to new information.

### Two-Spirit Identities—First Nations, North America

As least 150 pre-colonial Native American tribes acknowledged third genders in their communities (HRC Staff, 2020) and many Native American nations recognized five distinct genders. The roots of a limited and more restrictive gender binary can often be traced to colonization.

"Two spirit" is an umbrella term, originally introduced in 1990 in Winnipeg, Canada as a means of unifying various gender identities and expressions (Enos, 2018). However, individual nations and tribes have distinct names for gender-expansive people, for example, the *winkte* among the Lakota and the *nadleeh* among the Navajo people (Enos, 2018). Two-spirit people could often move freely between men and women and many held important leadership and spiritual roles in their nations.

Colonization and other acts of violence against Native peoples resulted in the tragic loss of many Native traditions including two-spirit identities. However, there is a growing revitalization and resistance movement among two-spirit people and other LGBTQ+ Native people throughout North America to revive two-spirit roles and traditions (Indian Health Service, n.d.).

## The Kathoey in Thailand

Legend suggests that the Thai system was always based on a model of the three genders: male, female, and kathoey (Holcomb, 2021). Kathoey are identified as male at birth and then transition to a feminine identity. This transition often occurs before puberty and is permanent. The kathoey are recognized as a socially acceptable identity.

Thailand is credited as being the most LGBTQ+ friendly country in East Asia (Mancino, 2019). There are three primary reasons for this. First is the presence of the kathoey: one in 166 men identify as kathoey (Mancino, 2019). The second reason is based on Thailand's history. Thailand is the only nation in the region to resist European colonization. Because of this resistance, they were able to hold onto their own cultural values and were less influenced by Eurocentric powers including normative heterosexuality and binary gender. Third, Thailand is a Buddhist country, and a major tenant of Buddhism is acceptance.

Many kathoey work in entertainment, singing, performing, and acting. While the kathoey often experience marginalization professionally, there is a wider spread social acceptance of the kathoey than what is seen in the West. Several kathoeys hold prominent professional positions including Dr. Seri Wongmontha, Tanwarin Sukkhapisit, and Prempreeda Pramoj Na Ayutthaya who, in addition to their activism, serve in academics, politics, and for the United Nations Educational, Scientific, and Cultural Organization program, respectively. Several kathoey have also achieved national fame, including Treechada Petcharat, an actress and model who won several beauty pageants in 2004, and Parinya Charoenphol, a famous boxer.

## Hijra in India

Drawing on verse from *The Ramayana*, which dates back to fourth century B.C., the Hindu legend said that when Lord Rama was exiled from Ayodhya, he told his disciples: "Men and women, please wipe your tears and go away." And so most left. However, a group of people who were neither men nor women stayed behind, at the edge of the forest (Gettleman, 2018). They were hijras, a specific gender identity. Many believe they have the power to bless or curse, which leads to social interactions mixed with both fear and entertainment. Although they are nationally recognized, hijra also have very few employment options. They are often forced to beg, crash ceremonies, or engage in sex work.

Hundreds of years ago, hijra were respected as a unique and valued group. However, when the British colonized India in the mid-1800s, they brought with them a strict and limiting belief system about sex, gender, and identity. Many scholars point to this as the start of homophobia and trans-discrimination in India (Gettleman, 2018). The hijra, who are not the only trans community in India, have specific cultural and community practices, including their own language, Hijra Farsi, which is a combination of Persian and Hindustani (Johari, 2014).

There have been some improvements for hijra in recent years. For example, confirmation surgeries can now be performed at some government hospitals. Further, transgender people are now recognized as an official third gender and are therefore eligible for social benefits including welfare. There is a wide vocabulary for gender identities (see: *Kinnar, Aravani*, and *Thirunangi*), and this nuance matters, as we know that much of the nuance is lost in attempting to translate this vocabulary for gender identities to English words or Western understandings. Finally, it is important to note that not all transgender people in India are also hijra.

## Closing Thoughts

In this lesson, you explored the expansive nature of gender and gender identity. This expansiveness spans across time, geography, and culture. The vast range of experiences may have reinforced what you knew about gender, rejected what you knew about gender, and even introduced new ideas about what it means to be human. Take a reflective beat to respond to the following in your journal:

- ◆ What challenged you in this lesson?
- ◆ What inspired you in this lesson?
- ◆ What are you taking away from this lesson?

## Unit 2—We Can All be Changemakers for Justice

What do you think of when you read the word *justice*? Your prior knowledge and lived experiences with equity, law, social justice, and the justice system may all affect your answer to this question. These complicated and varied answers matter. They also shed important light into the gaping distance between justice as a philosophy of love (see later) and practices that in the name of justice cause further harm and inequities. The United Nations Department of Economic and Social Affairs (2017) defines social justice as "the peaceful and prosperous coexistence within and among nations." What would it mean to have a peaceful and prosperous coexistence within and among all genders, peoples, and communities? Asked differently, what would it look like to live in a just world? As a scholarly community, these lessons ask you to wrestle deeply with this question and then strive wholeheartedly to make that vision a reality.

---

**Key Term: *Justice***

Feminist scholar and social justice advocate bell hooks (CNN—bell hooks, 2000) once said, "The greatest movement for social justice our country has ever known is the civil rights movement and it was totally rooted in a love ethic."

Justice in its deepest sense is rooted in radical, inclusive love. In its purest form it is fairness, equity, and humanity.

- ◆ How can fairness, equity, and a "love ethic" affirm humanity and free people from oppression (see the start where you are activity on p. 31)?

Tragically, many unjust things have been done in the name of justice. For this reason, it is essential to think critically about both philosophy and practice. In exploring justice work, you can use these questions as a starting place for analysis:

- ◆ What does justice mean in this context? Who is defining it?
- ◆ Is this practice furthering ethics and equity? If not, is it really justice?

In the following lessons, we encourage you to unpack these layers, asking critical questions about how we can each teach and learn toward a more just world.

---

**Related Term:** *Racial Justice*

Racial justice seeks to repair the intergenerational trauma inflicted on communities of color. This work includes dismantling systemic racism and the structures that perpetuate racism and ongoing harm toward communities of color. Racial justice is grounded in action, advocacy, and antiracist education, which moves purposefully toward new sustainable systems and practices rooted in racial equity.

## Lesson 1: "Ain't I A Woman?"—Sojourner Truth

More than 100 years after her passing, Sojourner Truth's legacy continues to influence justice work. She is revered as an influential feminist and abolitionist. Her work influenced Black feminisms (see Lesson 3 in this Unit), intersectionality (see Units 3 and 4 and the proseminar on pp. 162–173), and ongoing abolition work (see Lesson 1 in Unit 5). In the following reading, you will learn more about Truth's life, her advocacy, and a few allies who supported her along the way. You will then analyze Truth's most famous speech, "Ain't I A Woman?" (1851).

| Term | Definition |
| --- | --- |
| Advocacy | The act of supporting and working toward a specific cause, which can include organizing, educating, lobbying, training, and mobilizing. |
| Allyship | The active and intentional practice of being for a person or group of people to which you do not belong. Generally, allyship is when a person with more privilege or power in a specific area acts for or on behalf of those who are systematically marginalized or disempowered in that area. Allies continue to take action even when they are unsure of the outcome and/or when acting on behalf of this group carries personal risk. Allyship is about justice and (We continue this discussion in Unit 4.) |

### Sojourner Truth (1797–1883)

Isabella Bomfree, who later changed her name to Sojourner Truth, was born into slavery at the end of the 18th century. Subjected to violence, abuse, and the dehumanizing practices of slavery, Truth was bought and sold several times throughout her childhood and young adult life. Additionally, she faced the trauma and cruelty of watching both her parents and children sold away from her.

**Allyship—Shelter, Financial, and Legal Resources**

The year before New York legislation ended slavery, Truth escaped with her youngest daughter to the shelter of Maria and Isaac Van Wagener, an abolitionist couple. The Van Wageners took Truth in and purchased freedom for her and her youngest daughter. They also helped her successfully sue for the return of her young son Peter who had been illegally sold into slavery (Michels, 2015). This was one of Truth's first experiences with legislative advocacy, a strategy she used in her work for racial and gender justice throughout her life. As an advocate she went by the name Sojourner Truth, but she changed her legal name to Isabella Van Wagener (National Abolition Hall of Fame and Museum, n.d.).

## Legal Action and Advocacy Work

- ◆ During the Civil War, Truth organized supplies for Black troops and supported the Union cause.
- ◆ Following the war, she was honored with an invitation from President Abraham Lincoln to come to the White House.
- ◆ In Washington, D.C., she worked with the Freedmen's Bureau to support formerly enslaved people find jobs.
- ◆ She lobbied against segregation, including winning a case against a streetcar conductor who had violently blocked her from riding.
- ◆ Truth also collected thousands of signatures on a petition to provide formerly enslaved people with land; however, Congress never took action on this petition.

### Allyship—Amplifying Voices

In 1850, Sojourner Truth dictated her memoir *The Narrative of Sojourner Truth* to Olive Gilbert. In addition to writing the memoir, Gilbert also assisted Truth with the publication of the book. Truth was able to live off her book royalties (Michels, 2015).

Although Truth never had access to the educational opportunities to learn to read or write, she navigated the legal system, advocated passionately, and lectured widely on abolitionist and women's rights causes, championing suffrage and racial justice. She also spoke both Dutch, her native language, and English.

Sojourner Truth believed that racial justice and women's rights were inexorably linked. Truth taught that racial justice would never be fully achieved until people fought as tirelessly for women's rights as they did for other justice causes. She frequently reminded audiences and advocates that Black women were half of the formerly enslaved and enslaved populations. She also stressed that abolition alone was not equivalent with freedom and liberation—the fight for justice must continue with a focus on resisting racism, promoting literacy, overcoming sexism, and eradicating all forms of prejudice. This work and Truth's legacy continue today.

## Dialogue and Connect

- ◆ What examples of advocacy work can you identify in this reading? As you think about your own advocacy, what can you learn from Sojourner Truth?
- ◆ Review the definition of allyship. Why do you think the authors note that *allyship is about justice and not personal gain*, and how does that relate to this narrative?

## "Ain't I A Woman?"

Sojourner Truth delivered her most famous speech, "Ain't I A Woman?" in 1851. Below is an excerpt from the most cited version of her speech which appeared in her autobiography. Read the excerpt and respond to the questions that follow.

> That man over there says that women need to be helped into carriages, and lifted over ditches, and to have the best place everywhere. Nobody ever helps me into carriages, or over mud-puddles, or gives me any best place! And ain't I a woman?
>
> Look at me! Look at my arm! I have ploughed and planted, and gathered into barns, and no man could head me! And ain't I a woman?
>
> I could work as much and eat as much as a man—when I could get it—and bear the lash as well! And ain't I a woman?
>
> I have borne thirteen children, and seen most all sold off to slavery, and when I cried out with my mother's grief, none but Jesus heard me! And ain't I a woman?

## Think, Pair, Share

- ◆ Summarize Sojourner's Truth message in your own words. Why is this message important for both racial and gender justice?
- ◆ In 2014, bell hooks (see Lesson 3) published a book after Sojourner Truth's famous speech. Her book, titled *Ain't I a woman: Black Women and Feminism*, centers the experiences of Black women and explores the intersection of racism, sexism, and discrimination as they have impacted Black women throughout U.S. history. Why do you think bell hooks chose to reference Sojourner Truth's speech in her title? In what ways does Truth's message continue to have relevance today?

**Lesson 2: If Not You, Who? Sowing the Seeds of Advocacy**

**Thought Question**

◆ Who can work for the causes of gender justice and equity?

◆ How do gender stereotypes affect you and your peers?

In this lesson, scholars will analyze two speeches both calling for greater participation in feminist movements, "We Should All Be Feminists" by Chimamanda Adichie and "HeforShe" by Emma Watson. After listening to both speeches, encourage scholars to react, compare, contrast, and respond to these ideas. Both speeches are given by younger women focusing on contemporary perspectives; however, the lesson closes by looking back at our ancestors as scholars interview an elder in their communities. We (Kathryn and Jill) hope this juxtaposition leads to an analysis of the circular, cyclical, and forward movement of advocacy work.

### "HeforShe" Speech—Emma Watson, United Nations

In 2014, Emma Watson, British actor and UN Women Goodwill Ambassador, co-hosted a special event for the UN Women's HeForShe campaign. In this speech, Watson discusses how gender equality is everyone's issue and how gender stereotypes limit us all. The HeForShe campaign encourages men and boys to take up the issues of gender equality and equity as passionately as their women and girl counterparts.

### Listen to Watson's "HeforShe" Speech

Review Watson's speech—both the written transcript and video are available in our section appendix. After reviewing the speech, turn to a peer and discuss your reactions, reflections, and questions together.

◆ Which of Adichi's examples resonated with you?

◆ What would you challenge, refute, or qualify in this speech?

◆ What connections can you make to this speech?

### "We Should All be Feminists"—Chimamanda Adichie

Chimamanda Adichie, a Nigerian activist and author, gave a widely-watched TED Talk called "We Should All Be Feminists." She later published a book under the same title. Explore this work by listening to her talk or reading the book or transcript version with your peers.

**Discuss these questions as a class community:**

- ◆ Which of her examples resonated with you?
- ◆ What would you challenge, refute, or qualify in this speech?
- ◆ What personal connections can you make to this speech?
- ◆ Compare and contrast Adichie and Watson's speeches about feminism.
- ◆ How is Adichie's definition similar or different from what you thought feminism meant?

## A Feminist Lineage

Adichie (2014) said:

> My great grandmother, from the stories I've heard, was a feminist. She ran away from the house of the man she did not want to marry, and ended up marrying the man of her choice. She refused, she protested, she spoke up whenever she felt she's being deprived of access, of land, that sort of thing. My great grandmother did not know that word "feminist," but it doesn't mean that she wasn't one. More of us should reclaim that word.
>
> (p. 47–48)

Like Adichie's grandmother, many of our grandparents might not have called themselves feminists either, yet many engaged in important justice work that led to the opportunities their ancestors enjoy today. Below are a few examples to get you thinking:

- ◆ The great grandmother who escaped violence in her home country to start a new life in a place with more opportunities and safety for her children
- ◆ The great grandparents who stretched resources, sacrificed, and insisted that their daughter be the first in their family to attend college
- ◆ The great grandmother who wasn't able to attend school past sixth grade and who taught her children to read
- ◆ The great grandmother who joined a union to fight for equal pay after World War 2
- ◆ The grandparents who couldn't legally marry their partners of many decades (due to race, or sexuality, or both) and who taught their children about the power of love and hope
- ◆ The grandmother who raised dozens of children, including kin and foster youth, keeping young people safe and fed

- ◆ The grandparents who set up a community center or after school program that is still attended by youth today
- ◆ The grandmother who used her love of quilting to give hundreds of blankets to people experiencing homelessness in her city
- ◆ The grandmother who experienced housing and food insecurity in her youth and who now works in a health clinic addressing racial disparities in mental health

These elders are integral to your feminist lineage. Their sacrifice, values, convictions, and smarts are part of what brought you to this moment.

## Gender Advocate Interview

The world you live in is different from the world your great grandmother lived in. Consider how your ancestors and those in the generations before you helped move the cause of justice forward. Brainstorm the names of gender advocates you know who are two to three generations older than you. You might think of family members or community members. You may be able to immediately think of someone in your life who protested against gender-based job discrimination, wrote justice articles for a local newspaper, provided shelter to someone leaving an abusive relationship, ran a soup kitchen for those experiencing food insecurity, welcomed refugees, or were the first in their family to step boldly into a new space. You may need some reflective space to think about who you want to interview and what stories of justice, advocacy, or survival you want to learn about through this assignment. Speaking with other family members may help point you to just the right person.

### Gender Advocacy Is Expansive

Throughout this book, we (Kathryn and Jill) challenge scholars to consider how issues such as food insecurity, climate change, poverty, and infrastructure are essential feminist issues. The ways communities of color, Indigenous peoples, girls and women, and the LGBTQIA+ community are disproportionately affected by global issues, inequities, and structures are a critical lens for gender advocates to adopt as they seek ways to make a positive difference in their local and global communities.

Further, these lessons, and this activity, recognize that not all advocacy work is public or loud. Power and privilege directly impact the access people have to speak publicly or protest safely on behalf of issues that matter to them. This assignment celebrates that survival, love, and healing can all be critical acts of advocacy.

## Brainstorm Interview Questions

Working with a partner, brainstorm some ideas about the types of questions you might want to ask during your interview. What does advocacy or justice mean to them? What memories or stories could they tell you? What changes in gender justice have they witnessed during their lifetime? What changes are they hoping for in the future? When you are brainstorming your ideas, write open-ended instead of closed-ended questions. For example, instead of asking, "Was it hard being a woman and owning your own business?" ask open-ended questions like, "What challenges did you face as a woman owning a business?" or "What are you most proud of as a woman who owns her own business?"

## Conduct Your Interview

Decide how you are going to conduct your interview—a phone call, personal visit, over Zoom? When you conduct your interview, remember that you are there to listen and learn. Make eye contact; ask follow-up questions; and communicate, both verbally and nonverbally, that you are interested in what your interviewee is saying. It is also a good idea to take notes, and you may want to ask for permission to record the conversation. After you have conducted the interview, synthesize your notes by writing down the most interesting and important points you would like to share with your class about your conversation. Also consider how you will use the information you gained to be a gender advocate of your generation.

## Presentation

Tell your classmates about your interview. Who is the person you interviewed? What are their most significant and inspiring contributions? What did you learn from them about advocacy and justice? End your presentation by sharing with your class how you will apply the lessons you learned in this interview to your own life.

## ⏸ Take a Reflective Beat

Reflect on you and your peers' presentations. What did they teach about the expansive nature of advocacy? How does this rich history inform our current work for a more just world?

## Lesson 3: Feminisms Are for Everybody—Featured Scholar bell hooks

**Teaching Notes**

This lesson opens with an introductory text on differentiating feminisms. These distinctions are heady and academic. Review the text ahead of time to decide if its complexity is appropriate for your class. More advanced readers and those with some background in feminism already may want to read this text as is as a reading comprehension for discussion. Scholars for whom these concepts are brand new or those who have less experience with highly academic texts may benefit from a teacher summary of this information instead. If that is the case, share with your scholars the following key points:

1. Some scholars are moving away from the wave metaphor because it oversimplifies the feminist movements and may put generations against each other (e.g. my feminism is better than my mother's or grandmother's).
2. There are different frameworks within the feminist movement including liberal feminisms which work within systems to improve them; radical feminisms, which seek to create new systems that are more just; and Black feminisms which explore the ways multiple identities and oppressions work together and which critique the ways racism has further marginalized communities of color even with feminist movements.

## Feminisms—An Extremely Abridged Academic Introduction

Feminist movements, particularly in the United States, are often referenced in four waves. In brief, the first wave (1848–1920) is said to have focused on voting, property rights, and the abolition of slavery; the second wave (1960–1980) focused on equality, discrimination, and a rethinking of women's roles in both society and the home; the third wave (1990–2010) challenged assumptions of gender, sexuality, and beauty and complicated our understandings of identity and oppression through intersectionality; and the fourth wave (2010-present) utilizes the internet and media to advocate against sexual harassment and rape culture and for LGBTQIA+ rights, disability rights, and body positivity. While you will likely see references to these distinct waves in your reading, many scholars have moved away from this metaphor saying that it (1) discredits our global and historical movement toward equality as continuous and persistent, (2) positions the generations as against each other, and (3) oversimplifies the diversity of experiences that informed and continue to inform the movements for gender justice (Laughlin et al., 2010). For this reason, when we differentiate between feminisms in our lessons, we strive to do so by their unique theoretical, historical, and cultural contexts that are often overlapping and sometimes in conversation, conflict, or cooperation with each other.

| Term | Definition |
|---|---|
| Liberal feminism | A framework that operates *within* systems to improve them. Cornerstones of this framework include working toward equal opportunity, access, individual rights, liberty, and legislative equity (Fishman-Weaver, 2017). Establishing better sexual harassment or equal opportunity hiring practices are examples of initiatives that liberal feminists might advocate for. |
| Radical feminism | A framework that operates *beyond* systems to construct new structures and possibilities. Radical feminists believe that our systems are so deeply rooted in inequity and oppression they must be fundamentally deconstructed, reimagined, and built anew. A famous radical feminist text is Audre Lorde's essay "The Master's Tools Will Never Dismantle the Master's House" (2015). |
| Black feminisms | This framework centers the experiences of Black women while exploring the ways multiple identities and oppressions intersect to create contextualized experiences and conditions within systems. Black feminisms work concurrently on eradicating racism and sexism in the work toward a more just world. (See especially Sojourner Truth, Kimberlé Crenshaw, Angela Davis, and bell hooks.) |
| Queer theory | A critical framework that challenges power dynamics related to gender and sexuality. Queer theory rejects essentialist (or pre-determined) definitions and binary thinking. Rather than assuming that categories of gender, sex, and sexuality are natural and fixed, queer theorists seek a more nuanced understanding of gender as dynamic and negotiated. This framework celebrates a full spectrum of identities. Queer theory frameworks are used in literary criticism, political criticism, sociology studies, and more layered accounts of history. (See especially Gloria Anzaldúa, Adrienne Rich, Judith Butler, and Eve Kosofsky Sedgwick.) |

## bell hooks—Foundations of Knowledge

These frameworks and ideologies shape how you view the world and the approaches you take toward bringing about positive change. In the next section of this lesson, you will explore your own beliefs about knowledge production through the work of bell hooks, a thought leader in *Black feminisms*.

Gloria Jean Watkins (1952–2021) published under the pseudonym bell hooks.[5] This name honored her maternal great grandmother. hooks used a lowercase version of the name to emphasize that the focus is on the work, not the person. A prolific author and feminist scholar, bell hooks' work explores race, class, gender, identity, education, and critical consciousness.

hooks proudly identified as a Black, queer feminist scholar. Her work encouraged love, healing, and finding new ways to live and come together. These beliefs were grounded in her queer identity. hooks defined queerness as "the self that is at odds with everything around it and has to invent and create and find a place to speak and to thrive and to live" (Ibrahim, 2021, para 3). In 1983 (republished in 2014), she wrote *Feminist Theory: From Margins to Center* (hooks, 2014b), which called on scholars and activists to engage in feminism that recognized the ways racism, classism, and sexism worked as cooperative webs of oppression. Her vision for justice is one that ends sexist exploitation and oppression while working with the same diligence to end other systems of oppression including racism.

| Term | Definition |
|---|---|
| Critical consciousness | An ability to see and understand inequities in our communities and a commitment to take action against injustices. |
| Patriarchy | A system of government, society, or family in which men hold power and women are systematically excluded from power. Feminist movements seek to dismantle patriarchal systems and establish more equitable systems. |

### Scholarly Connections

 **Thought Questions**

- ◆ Where did you learn about gender, inclusion, and sexism?
- ◆ Were these concepts that someone specifically taught you or were they things you picked up on through your lived experiences?

In the next activity, you will have the opportunity to think deeply about gender and advocacy work. Read and respond to the quotes below. These quotes are from Chapter 4 of bell hooks' book *Feminism is for Everybody* (2020). This chapter outlines some of hooks' ideology about education and critical consciousness.

> Most of us had been socialized by parents and society to accept sexist thinking. We had not taken time to figure out the roots of our perceptions (p. 19).

- What have you learned about gender, sexism, discrimination, and equality from your families and other spaces like school, faith communities, and sports?
- How have you or other people you know been taught to accept sexist thinking? What does that look like?

> By failing to create a mass-based educational movement to teach everyone about feminism we allow mainstream patriarchal mass media to remain the primary place where folks learn about feminism, and most of what they learn is negative (p. 23).

- What does the media teach young people about gender and feminism? Are those lessons positive, negative, or a combination of both? How so?

> We need work that is especially geared towards youth culture. No one produces this work in academic settings (p. 23).

- Why is work with young people so important?
- What work can young people do to resist discrimination and sexism?

# Concept Synthesis Project—WGST & Me

Name _____ Date_____

Over the last two units, you have started to learn about the breadth of WGST as well as different feminist frameworks. Depending on how your class community organized your WGST learning, you may have completed several or all of the following activities:

| Activating Prior Knowledge—Feminist T-Shirt Design |
|---|
| **UNIT 1: Feminist Theory—Introduction** |
| Lesson 1: SDG 5—Target Research |
| Lesson 2: Start Where You Are—Thought Work on WGST and Feminism |
| Lesson 3: Scholar Study—Sojourner Truth |
| **UNIT 2: We Can All Be Changemakers for Justice** |
| Lesson 1: Gender-Expansive Identity Readings |
| Lesson 2: Feminist Speech Analysis (Emma Watson and Chimamanda Adichie) |
| Lesson 3: Feminisms and Critical Consciousness Thought Work (bell hooks) |

Take some time to go through your own growing body of WGST work. Look for trends, areas for further exploration, and ideas you are proud of.

**You have important things to say.**
- ◆ What issues are you drawn to?
- ◆ What questions do you want to explore next?
- ◆ What scholars, leaders, and frameworks did you resonate with?

As we close out these units, synthesize your own growing framework for gender advocacy into a culminating project. Choose one of the following prompts and craft a thoughtful response. Your response may build directly on one of the activities you started in this unit or it may be a completely new product.

**Synthesis Prompts**
- ◆ How can young people persist in the fight for justice, representation, equity, and inclusion? Give specific local and global examples.

◆ What are the differences between equality and equity? How do these concepts relate to our work as WGST scholars?
◆ Identify local organizations in your communities who are doing important advocacy work around issues of gender, representation, and inclusion? How can you support these efforts?

Present your response in a poster, essay, skit, mini-documentary, or editorial. Below are some guidelines to consider as you work on your synthesis project.

| Title and medium | What is the title of your work? What is the meaning of that title? In this project, you have the creative latitude to use any kind of medium you want (e.g. music, art, videography, essay writing, etc.). Why did you choose the medium you did? |
|---|---|
| Thesis | What is the main message of your project? What do you want readers or viewers to learn or experience when they read or see your work? |
| Feminist theory | How does your project connect to one or more of the feminist theories or key vocabulary we learned in these units? What ideas are you building on or illustrating? Note: When you draw on another scholar's work, it is important to give them credit by citing their work. |
| Course Theme(s) | How does your project illustrate or show a commitment to resistance, representation, or radical hope? Be specific. |
| Inspiration | Whose shoulders are you standing on? How have your own lived experiences contributed to the issues you are reporting on and care about? |

## Extension Exercises for Concept 1

### Deconstructing the Gender Box—Creative Challenge
The gender box is a metaphor often used to illustrate the ways binary thinking limits identity and behavior.

| Term | Definition |
|---|---|
| Gender box | Gender roles that are prescribed or constructed by society. |
| Binary thinking | Believing there are only two possibilities. |

Think about a more inclusive visual of gender than a box and create an artistic representation of what that might look like. Some ideas are amorphous shapes, Venn diagrams, and spectrums. Because you are literally *thinking outside the box* here, feel free to come up with your own creative ideas!

- ◆ What expansive possibilities did you most resonate within thinking through this activity?
- ◆ How can you take this activity from an art or thinking task to action and application?

### Children's Book
Create a children's book that explains WGST in a way that elementary-aged children would understand. Another idea is to create a children's book of one of the key figures or pivotal moments in feminist history.

### Snap Interview
Do snap interviews with ten people asking these questions:

- ◆ How would you define WGST?
- ◆ How would you define *feminism*?
- ◆ What are feminist accomplishments from the past 100 years?
- ◆ Are you a feminist? Why or why not?

### Take Back the Night March
Research *Take Back the Night March*es against sexual assault and plan a Take Back the Night march or rally to raise awareness of and protest sexual assault. (See teaching notes on pp. 22–23 for some tips on addressing this difficult issue in the classroom.)

### A Mantra for Moving Past Imposter Syndrome
Toward the end of her speech to the United Nations, Emma Watson references a common feeling called *imposter syndrome*.

| Term | Definition |
| --- | --- |
| Imposter syndrome | A feeling or belief that you aren't qualified for the tasks you have been asked to do. |

She also commits to moving forward even as she wonders if she is the right person for the task. "If not me, who, if not now, when . . . I don't know if I am qualified to be here. All I know is that I care about this problem. And I want to make it better" (United Nations, 2014).

Imposter syndrome is common and can happen anywhere. You might experience it in class, on the field, in your extracurriculars, or anywhere you are called to do something challenging or just out of your comfort zone. Recognizing and normalizing imposter syndrome can be a source of strength. While imposter syndrome can feel deeply personal, it is also important to look at these feelings through some of the lenses introduced in these lessons. Often feelings of imposter syndrome are triggered by racism, classism, sexism, and homophobia. Continued work toward justice and equity is essential in cultivating spaces that are inclusive and brave.

Throughout these units, you will be asked to identify issues you care deeply about, to advocate to make your communities more just and inclusive, and to share personal stories. All of these tasks require courage. As you practice bravery and navigate the big feelings that come with doing courageous tasks, it may help to have some language and strategies for addressing imposter syndrome.

Think about an area in your life where you feel or have felt imposter syndrome. Try this mantra and keep it in mind whenever you need a little boost.

"If not me, who, if not now, when. I belong in this

_____
(class/activity/leadership role)

I care about _____. And can do this."
(why you are in this class/activity/role)

### Key Figures

In our "Beyond the Binary" lesson, scholars learn more about the kathoey, the hijra, and two-spirit people. However, the lessons do not go into depth into specific key figures. As an extension, identify and research a key figure from any of these identity groups. The links in our chapter appendix offer a helpful starting place.

**Helpful Links**
- Sojourner Truth's "Ain't I a Woman?" speech available on Learning for Justice: www.learningforjustice.org/classroom-resources/texts/aint-i-a-woman
- *The New York Times*: The Peculiar Position of India's Third Gender (note this article discusses sex work): www.nytimes.com/2018/02/17/style/india-third-gender-hijras-transgender.html
- 12 Incredible Indigenous LGBTQ Women and Two-Spirit People You Should Know: www.autostraddle.com/12-awesome-native-american-and-first-nation-lgbtq-women-and-two-spirit-people-311473/
- Emma Watson's HeforShe Speech—Video: www.youtube.com/watch?v=gkjW9PZBRfk
- Emma Watson's "HeforShe Speech"—Transcript: www.unwomen.org/en/news/stories/2014/9/emma-watson-gender-equality-is-your-issue-too
- HeforShe Alliance webpage—www.heforshe.org/en
- Chimamanda Adichie—We Should All Be Feminists: www.ted.com/talks/chimamanda_ngozi_adichie_we_should_all_be_feminists
- Kamala Harris Acceptance Speech: www.youtube.com/watch?v=-ExPm_hJQYpQ
- 7 Historic Firsts that Prove Representation Matters in Politics: www.wellandgood.com/representation-in-politics/

## Notes

[1] While the focus quote belongs to one bright young person, out of respect for their identity and privacy, "Mae" is a composite of a few different young people I've worked and learned with.

[2] The prefix *trans* comes from Latin meaning across, beyond, or on the other side of.

[3] If scholars would like some help getting started, we have provided an example chart in the chapter appendix.

[4] Recognizing these limitations, we (Kathryn and Jill) worked specifically with scholars more familiar with the cultural backgrounds of India and Thailand in this lesson.

[5] bell hooks passed away while we (Kathryn and Jill) were writing this book. We both felt this loss. I (Kathryn) had the honor of meeting hooks during my undergraduate years when she visited the Women's and Gender Studies department where I was studying and met with student leaders over pizza. Both Jill and I treasured her books, including her children's books, which we read to our children.

# 2

# Intersectionality

## Advisory Editor Concept Foreword
## by Dr. Adrian Clifton

*Dr. Adrian Chanel Clifton (she/her) is a proud alum of the University of Missouri-Columbia. While attending the university, she earned three degrees: a Bachelor of Science degree in elementary education, a master's degree in curriculum and instruction, and a doctoral degree in the area of learning, teaching, and curriculum. Dr. Clifton served as the first College of Education alum to teach abroad at a Mizzou Academy international partner school. It was an honor for both Dr. Clifton and her family to live in Brazil and experience their culture firsthand. Dr. Clifton has a background in poetry, hip hop, and fashion. She finds creative ways to connect her love of the arts to her students and the communities she serves.*

At what intersections do you reside? What borders have you crossed? How do your identities (gender, sexual orientation, race, faith, ability, and socio-economic status) influence your everyday experiences? When has your race identity dictated the food you have access to? This is an example of the deep-rooted questions scholars will dig into in their study of *intersectionality*.

DOI: 10.4324/9781003323327-3

I first wrote about intersectionality in my dissertation in 2016. I used autoethnography to study the experiences of five Black women and girls, including myself, who were living at the intersections of race and poverty in Columbia, Missouri. In addition to radical hope, I discovered the power that came from radical faith and radical relationships within radical community spaces. These ingredients were, and still are, vital for our survival.

Black women and girls are disproportionately affected by health disparities, including limited access to mental health services and early childcare options, as well as systemic inequities in educational practices and the welfare system (Love, 2020). School systems are burdened, and Black girls are often subjected to harsh and unequal discipline policies that often push them out of school and into juvenile detention and adult prison institutions (Love, 2019; Morris, 2018). Yet, it was at this same intersection where the Black girls in my study woke and rose for the day unapologetically. As a Black woman researcher, I was intrigued and curious about this "rose out of concrete"[1] mentality, even within myself.

My research led me to the fertilizer and water source for such roses. This radical community space was beyond concrete walls ordained in graffiti, past a bridge blaring with sirens, and just beyond yellow caution tape marking the third murder of the summer. There, in the Columbia Housing projects, stood a brick home blooming with flowers kindridly known as Granny's House. Inside this space, Black girls read about their worth in biblical texts, studied for exams, ate dinner, and prayed before stepping out to cross the busy intersection leading home. This space was a lifeline for the girls and me. Granny's House is run by Pam and Dr. Ellis Ingram. "Granny Pam," as she is known to the whole city, shared stories and wisdom to help us navigate our lives and release and heal our traumas.

When I think about the complexities of intersectionality, I am reminded of Kat, who at the time of my study, was a 16-year-old enthusiastic Black girl who wore her hair in a tight bun at the top of her head, religiously. Kat was a freshman at Hickman High School and the star player of the girls basketball team. Colleges were already seeking her out. But many games, Kat played with a hungry stomach. During her sophomore year, her mother was evicted from their home. She spent nights on my couch when I lived in an apartment in public housing.

In 2017, I got my first university position and moved into my first home. As a mother of four, Kat continued to come over to babysit for me. We held ice cream cones in our hands and made a toast on my behalf: "For movin' on up in the world, Dr. A!" Kat exclaimed enthusiastically. I made her promise not to forget about "us small people" when she rose to become a famous philanthropist one day. Today Kat is making good on her promise. As a community activist in Kansas City, she is currently creating the blueprint for an ice cream shop in one of the toughest areas hit by crime. She will call it *Granny's House*. Kat and I shared radical faith within a radical relationship built at a radical community space.

As women, our lives are constantly being affected by intersections. In this proseminar, scholars will study the works of Patricia Hill Collins and the Combahee Collective River Statement, and they will engage in further research on their own identities and experiences and those of the people they have studied. Like crossing guards on a busy intersection, Kathryn and Jill safely walk scholars through definitions, analytics, and research, essential for students, educators, and activists to consider and think about critically. With a useful set of tools and references, scholars will be invited to create, celebrate, and connect to the world of justice work.

---

### Teaching Concept Overview—Intersectionality

**Purpose:** In these units, "Matrices and Margin" and "The Personal is Political, The Power of More Complete Stories," scholars learn about intersectionality (see Kimberlé Crenshaw); the complexities of *social space*; and the ways identities, experiences, and social issues are all informed by multiple and overlapping systems of power, privilege, and oppression. This work is informed by bell hooks' scholarship on *center and margins*, Patricia Hill Collins' *outsider within* construct, and the Combahee Collective River Statement, all of which we study directly. Building on this theoretical framework, scholars utilize these concepts to engage in praxis around food insecurity and health care. This includes research and action grounded in their local context. Additionally, scholars consider the danger of a single story (Adichie, 2009); study gendered impacts of climate change; and research key figures engaged in food, environmental, racial, and gender justice work. Scholars end the unit with an arts-integrated research and reflection activity that extends their learning on a key figure introduced in these units and celebrates the multiple identities and lived experiences that each scholar brings to our class communities.

✔ **Objectives: By the end of this unit, scholars will be able to:**

◆ Define *intersectionality* and how one's position in social space is influenced by systems of oppression.

◆ Analyze the Combahee River Collective Statement and connect those statements to Patricia Hill Collins' concepts from *Outsider Within*.

- Research and take action related to the United Nations' Sustainable Development Goal (SDG) 2 (zero hunger).
- Create an intersectional protocol for care.
- Think critically about the importance of multiple stories.
- Analyze the United Nations' SDG 13 to better understand the gendered impacts of climate change.
- Connect intersectionality and radical hope to justice work.

**? Essential Questions for Scholars**

- How are systems of oppression related across identities and social issues?
- How have the experiences and wisdom of Black and Indigenous women informed feminist and social justice scholarship?
- What is the connection between personal stories and broad global issues?

**Reflective Questions for Educators**

- How can I teach more complete stories across my curriculum?
- What does it mean to teach for radical hope?
- How can I support scholars in practicing solidarity and engaging in justice work in our communities?

**Activate Prior Knowledge—Womanism**

| Unit 3—Matrices and Margins | Unit 4—The Personal Is Political: The Power of More Complete Stories |
|---|---|
| Lesson 1—Center and Margins<br>Lesson 2—Systems of Oppression: *Outsider Within*<br>Lesson 3—Mother Earth: Gendered Impacts of Climate Change | Lesson 1—Chimamanda Ngozi Adichie: "The Danger of a Single Story"<br>Lesson 2—Food Insecurity: Why Hunger is an Intersectional and Feminist Issue<br>Lesson 3—Praxis, Food Insecurity: A Local Justice Issue<br>Lesson 4—Beverly Greene and Psychological Resistance |

**Synthesis—Intersectional Collage Compare and Contrast**

*Figure 2.1—Teaching Concept Overview*

## Concept 2—Dedications

**Kathryn's Dedication**—I would like to dedicate this chapter to Gabriella. I had the honor of having Gabriella in my classes for three years. She was a serious person with a big laugh. I connected with her right away. Gabriella joined our class a month after immigrating from Guatemala. Her family were Indigenous Mayans, and she grew up speaking Mam. When they began their immigration journey, Gabriella learned Spanish. In the United States, she lived in an apartment with her mom, auntie, sister, and cousins. At our predominantly Latinx school, Gabriella strengthened her Spanish and learned English. She served as a frequent translator across all three languages for the adults in her life, including me. Years before I learned about border-crossing theory (Douglas, 2013; Lopez et al., 2006),[2] Gabriella showed me the complexity and power of navigating across borders, boundaries, languages, and cultures. There were aspects of her personal narrative that she shared boldly in our class and other parts of her story she held close for her and her family. Gabriella spoke with gentle, deep wisdom. She led by example and was a friend to all.

Several times while writing this chapter, I thought of Gabriella. Her story, the parts of it she graciously shared with me, represent the heavy and bright themes in this chapter—racial justice, immigration policy, identity politics, translingualism, multiple marginality, resistance, and radical hope. Gabriella was eight years old when I met her and already a leader and a teacher. I continue to put my faith in the world that she and her peers, including your scholars, will lead.

**Jill's Dedication**—Sometimes we are the teachers, and sometimes we are the students. I (Jill) would like to dedicate this chapter to a group of wise women who are my teachers. I live in a rural town outside of Kansas City, Missouri, in a space where diversity and inclusion are not always celebrated. Nineteen miles away in South Kansas City, however, is an intersectional, small congregation of beautifully diverse, inclusive people, and in that space our family has made our spiritual home.

Dr. Martin Luther King Jr., who was a pastor in our church's denomination, once said that Sunday morning was the most segregated hour of the week. In contrast, he also dreamed of a "Beloved Community" that was a space of justice, inclusion, and equity. Sunday morning is far from a segregated hour at our church, and this group of people is a Beloved Community that works together towards racial justice, LGBTQIA+ inclusion, and equity for all. Some of the dearest people in my life are members of this church— Daylin and Dalie from Cuba; Dezo from Haiti; Mariko from Japan; and a host of diverse women from the Kansas City community: Stephanie, Geneva, Pat,

Susie, FoFo, Fortuna, Jessie, Lois, Margo, Jan, Melba, Dawn, Sandi, Laura, Melba, Diana, and Yvonne. These women have wrapped my children up in their extravagant love, mentored me in my spiritual and personal journey, and taught me much with their wisdom and their stories. Sometimes these stories are painful, such as when they tell stories of racial segregation when they were growing up or how their children have been racially profiled. Many times, these stories are full of care, such as an email I received last year when I was in the middle of a cancer scare from a dear woman whose subject of the email was simply "Love." Often, these stories are full of hope, and we celebrate joy together in graduations, weddings, babies, and intentional community movements that work toward justice and equity.

I believe that if we intentionally seek intersectional, inclusive community, we will experience Dr. Martin Luther King Jr's vision of a Beloved Community, and our classrooms can encompass that space in a community full of radical hope.

## Concept Introduction by Kathryn and Jill

"I will center Black women in this analysis in order to contrast the multidimensionality of Black women's experience with the single-axis analysis that distorts these experiences" (Crenshaw, 1989, p. 139).

Each person brings a unique constellation of gender, racial, ethnic, national, and linguistic identities. How are identities negotiated and socially constructed? Do our identities take on new meanings in new contexts? How is power negotiated within our various identities? Kimberlé Crenshaw explored many of these questions through a concept she called "intersectionality." As Crenshaw (1989) explains intersectionality:

> Consider an analogy to traffic in an intersection, coming and going in all four directions. Discrimination, like traffic through an intersection, may flow in one direction, and it may flow in another. If an accident happens in an intersection, it can be caused by cars traveling from any number of directions and, sometimes, from all of them. Similarly, if a Black woman is harmed because she is in an intersection, her injury could result from sex discrimination or race discrimination.
>
> (p. 149)

Much of Crenshaw's early work focused on the experiences of Black women in the United States. Crenshaw's seminal article on demarginalizing the intersection of race and gender (1989) explored how the courts interpreted the stories of Black women plaintiffs. Too often she found that the testimonies of Black women had a singular focus on either race or gender but not both and not the ways these multiple identities intersected. The result "essentially eras[es] Black women's distinct experiences" (p. 146). To use her term, *a single axis analysi*s of our identities is always incomplete and often misleading.

Crenshaw's framework illustrates the need for a more complex and holistic understanding of the ways our multiple identities, particularly our marginalized identities, work together. Multiple identities (e.g. race, class, gender, ethnicity, etc.) intersect to create complex and contextualized experiences in social space. These experiences are multidimensional.

---

 **Thought Questions**

- ◆ Which of your identities are most important?
- ◆ Which are least understood by others?
- ◆ How do your answers to these questions change depending on context?

---

Following are some thoughts on a few of my (Kathryn's) identities.

I am a woman, a daughter, a partner, and a sister. I was raised in a multifaith home—my children practice both Christian and Jewish traditions. My family is multiracial, which means we often have to announce both that we belong to each other and that we belong in certain spaces. I am fair skinned, far sighted, and suffer chronic migraines. I have a laugh that people often tell me is "too loud" for my 5'1" frame. I work in a top leadership position in education, a sector where women account for 70+% of teachers and less than 25% of top leadership positions (Superville, 2017). As a result, when people first see me, they assume I am a teacher and not a school administrator. I am an introvert and a poet. I do my best thinking when I have quiet time to think by myself and space to write my ideas out.

As you read about these identities, notice the ways race, gender, and experience are negotiated within my daily experiences and narrative. You can practice this exercise with the scholars in your class by having them list some their salient identities and pick out a few to elaborate on what those mean as I did with this sentence: *My family is multiracial, which means we often have to announce both that we belong to each other and belong in certain spaces.*

Not only are identities multidimensional; they are also influenced by our communities and circumstances. For example, the experiences of being a Black woman in the United States are different from what it means to be a

Black woman in Brazil or a Black woman in Nigeria. In the next two units, you will explore belonging, inclusion, identities, and social space. You will also explore how power and politics influence whose identities and stories are centered and celebrated and whose are excluded. As you are learning throughout this book, the identities and experiences of women, people of color, LGBTQIA+ individuals, and refugees and immigrants have all been historically and continuously underrepresented, misunderstood, and marginalized in mainstream spaces. The consequences of incomplete stories are serious and damaging. These next two units continue our work of celebrating more complete and more complex stories rooted in both resistance and radical hope.

## Educator Letter for Concept 2—*Are You Making Room for Joy?*

Dear Valued Educator,

In this connecting space, we (Kathryn and Jill) invite you to think with us about the upcoming chapter content. Make a cup of coffee, take a deep breath, and let's settle in together. Knowing that no one teaches, writes, or lives in a vacuum, we want to keep reminding you that your work matters. Finally, we want to explore what care might look like **for you** in teaching these complex and charged topics.

### Your Work Matters

These lessons affirm your scholars' identities. They address racial justice directly. They help cultivate brave spaces for story sharing and community. In these lessons, you have the opportunity to show young people that they matter, that their experiences are valid, and that the knowledge they bring to our classroom is important. This is deeply worthwhile work.

### Care Strategies for Educators

While writing this book, both Jill and I (Kathryn) were reading Amanda Gorman's poetry collection titled, *Call Us What We Carry* (2021). You can see the fingerprints of Gorman's poetry throughout this text. While thinking about care strategies for this section, I reflected on Gorman's title.

- ◆ **What are you carrying?** As you prepare for these next units on intersectionality, identity, race, gender, justice, and identity politics, what are you carrying? Where do you enter these lessons? When have you been an *outsider within* (Collins, 1986)? Which of your identities are centered, and which are marginalized (hooks, 1989)? Which do you celebrate, and which does your school community celebrate? (These may or may not be the same.) How have you and your communities been affected by health disparities, food insecurity, and climate change? Reflecting on the many layers of your own narrative can help you enter these lessons with nuance and perspective.

◆ **You don't have to carry everything alone.** A common theme across our care strategies is a reminder that this work happens best in the context of communities. We (Jill and Kathryn) encourage you to identify peers and support groups for you. Lean on your community as a source of support. No one teaches, learns, or lives in a vacuum. We've encouraged you to pool the collective energies and talents of those around you.

   – What are ways you can connect your personal communities to your work in the classroom?
   – Do you have an artist friend who could give a guest lesson on art projects?
   – Do you have a friend in the business sector who could donate materials or space for events?
   – Who are your friends' friends, and what connections do they have that might support your work? Consider nonprofits, politicians, and local leaders.
   – Would your local paper be willing to cover a learning event in your classroom?
   – Do you have an NPR member station that would invite young people to talk about their work?
   – Is there a health clinic or community center in town that would be willing to guest teach on wellness and health disparities?

The list goes on and on. These examples are real strategies that I (Kathryn) have used in my own classroom to get access to materials and experts and to shine a light on the important work my scholars are doing. Lean on your connections to leverage possibilities, to celebrate your class community, and to show your scholars that your classroom extends far beyond four physical walls.

◆ **Are you making space for joy?** As you practice care in these lessons, pay particular attention to the scholars who have the most risk in these lessons. Whose stories are being told, and how are they being told? Seek every opportunity to affirm and celebrate your scholars, particularly your Black, Indigenous, people of color (BIPOC) scholars who may find mirror narratives in the following units. As you engage in this teaching, conduct a *joy audit*. Do each of your lessons offer a celebration or moment of joy? BIPOC histories, cultures, and identities are more than oppression and discrimination. They are also joy, art, leadership, innovation, and brilliance. Welcome scholars to a vibrant celebration of ideas and use these moments of joy to buoy your class in their ongoing pursuit of justice.

With admiration,

Kathryn and Jill

## Activate Prior Knowledge—Womanism

 **Thought Questions**

◆ Why do names matter?
◆ Are there specific names people call you in specific situations?
◆ How did these names come to be?
◆ What role do they fill?
◆ Do you know what your name means?

I (Kathryn) am *Kat* to many of my closest friends. I am *Kathryn* or *KFW* at work. I am *Dr. Fishman-Weaver* in formal settings. I am *Dr. K* or *Dr. KFW* to my academic peers and college students. My aunts and grandma will always call me *Kathy*. In each of these situations, I am still me, but each name shines light on a different part of my identity or relationships. My parents named me *Kathryn* after my maternal great grandmother. My middle name *Eva* comes from my paternal great grandmother. Both women are known in our family history for their strength, smarts, and resistance to traditional gender norms. My last name is a combination of my original family name and my spouse's family name. We both hyphenated to honor our collective family lineages.

What does naming have to do with feminism? Personal names often have a lot to do with gender and gender roles. For example, the practice of women changing their names at marriage is linked to centuries old laws and practices about "coverture,"[3] ownership, and the restriction of women's rights. What about the name feminism itself? Although feminism is intended to be a movement to expand justice, historically, the feminist movements have left out and excluded women of color in general and Black women in particular. It is from this history that Alice Walker created a new word, a new name: *womanism*. Walker (1983) defined *womanism* this way:

> A black feminist or feminist of color. From the black folk expression of mothers to female children, "you acting womanish," i.e., like a woman. Usually referring to outrageous, audacious, courageous, or *willful* behavior. Wanting to know more and in greater depth than is considered "good" for one. . . . Responsible. In charge. *Serious*. . . . [A womanist is also] committed to survival and wholeness of entire people, male *and* female. . . . Womanist is to feminist as purple is to lavender.
>
> (p. xi-xii)

In response to the marginalization of women of color in feminist movements, Walker decided to name a new feminism. Womanism created a more inclusive space where women of color are centered rather than pushed to the margins. The name *womanism* actively addresses the intersection of sexism and racism in feminism. Womanists identified as feminist *and* preferred to use a different name. Many *Black feminisms* (see pp. 52) and woman of color feminisms were informed by womanism.

*Think, Pair, Share*
Think again about naming:

- ◆ Why do names matter?
- ◆ What is the power in naming or renaming?
- ◆ Why is the term *womanism* important in our WGST studies, and how does that relate to this conversation about naming?

# Unit 3—Matrices and Margin

In these units, you will learn about some of the ways that the feminist movement has left out key voices, particularly the voices from women of color, and you will learn about the powerful ways Black and Indigenous women of color (BIWOC) have spoken back and led (and continue to lead) the way toward greater justice and inclusion. This work is political, social, and personal. Creating spaces that are brave and expansive is essential to the fabric of our everyday experiences. In this unit, you will explore what inclusivity and safety mean at the grocery store, in the doctor's office, in the workplace, and at school. This type of analysis requires us to look deeply at identity, marginalization, and discrimination. Scholars consider the ways racism, heterosexism, ageism, ableism, sexism, and classism rob spaces, communities, and people of their vibrance and authenticity. Further, scholars will study how none of our identities and experiences exist in a social vacuum. In fact, for many individuals who are multiply marginalized (see Beverly Greene's work in Lesson 4 and our unit on maternal health (pp. 136–154), these experiences with discrimination are compounded.

For example, consider how Luiza, a hypothetical woman living in northwestern Iowa, is multiply marginalized in the following example. As a woman, Luiza experiences sexism at her neighborhood grocery store when men call out lewd comments to her, and because of this, she no longer feels safe shopping for groceries at night. As a Latina, she experiences racism when her neighbor tells her that her traditional cooking smells strange and that she should "go back home." As a queer woman, Luiza experiences heterosexism when her partner is not included in family events at her work. Finally, as a low-income woman, she experiences classism when the store clerk makes judging comments about her finances regardless of whether she pays with cash, credit, or check. These are small examples of a constellation of overt and covert aggressions that Luiza experiences daily.

These experiences are also compounding and layered. For example, when Luiza approached her boss at work about her partner not being invited to the recent social event where other spouses had been invited, her boss said he didn't know that Luiza was in a romantic relationship. He assumed the woman who picked her up each day and brought her lunch several afternoons a week was her sister. "I mean, you're both Mexican," he said. Neither she nor her partner are from Mexico, and Luiza often kisses her partner when she sees her.

Further, Luiza's experiences are not static. She has different challenges when she navigates the health care system as a queer Latina woman than when she enters the teachers' lounge in the predominately White school where she works as a paraprofessional. And when she and her son visit her grandparents in her home country of Argentina, she has yet another different set of experiences.

Working toward a more just world requires a complex understanding of the ways oppression, privilege, and identity are layered, contextualized, and intersectional. In the following unit, we explore bell hooks' work on *center and margins*, Patricia Hill Collins' work on being an *outsider within*, and Beverley Greene's work on *psychological resistance*. The unit includes two praxis projects. First, scholars will work to understand and address food insecurity in their local communities (pp. 95–97). Next, scholars will work in teams to interview a health professional, develop research questions, and engage in independent or team research on a related topic of their choosing (pp. 99–100). Both of these activities could take several class periods. If you do not want to dedicate this much class time to the projects, you can shorten the health protocol activity so that scholars only complete the pre-research protocol that is included in the book.

### Key Term—*Social Space*

All people occupy specific and contextualized positions in social space. Access to experiences, cultural knowledge, and resources influences the ease or difficulty we have in navigating different social spaces such as classrooms, community events, public places, and online forums such as social media. For example, the social and cultural capital needed to navigate a soccer game may be different than the social and cultural capital needed to navigate a college physics class or a neighborhood block party. Looking at a space through a feminist lens—meaning a lens for justice and inclusion—asks you to look for how different spaces affirm, welcome, and celebrate. It helps to get specific. For example, how is this computer science program affirming girls and women? How is this museum inclusive of African American stories? In what ways is this conference accessible to first-generation college students?

In her 2016 article on the famous astronaut Sally Ride, feminist scholar Mary Hunt shares that while Ride did incredible work to expand access to science education for girls and young women, she never felt safe enough to be public about her 30-year relationship with her same-gender partner. The onus to create safe space is on all of us. Hunt (2016) challenges, "What are we doing about the fact that we can visit outer space, but we cannot create enough social space to accommodate the range of ways people love?" As you work through these lessons, consider the ways social space is negotiated and challenged. Ask yourself how an intersectional analysis can help create spaces that are more affirming, inclusive, safe, and just.

### Lesson 1—Center and Margins

 **Thought Questions**

◆ What does it mean to be on the margins of something, such as a situation, group, or experience?

◆ What does it mean to be in the center of something?

◆ How are these two spaces different?

| Term | Definition |
|---|---|
| Margins | A concept to help us think about social space. The margins can be a philosophical or physical place (noun). Being in the margins is "to be part of the whole but outside the main body" (hooks, 2014b, p. xvii). This is where the verb *marginalize* comes from. |
| Center | A concept to help us think about social space. The center can be a philosophical or physical space (noun); however, *to center* can also be a verb meaning to be seen, heard, known, and celebrated. |

"Feminist theory lacks wholeness, lacks the broad analysis that could encompass a variety of human experiences."

(hooks, 2014b, p. xviii)

### Let's Draw It Out

Draw a circle in the middle of a piece of paper. Within the circle, write down the places and communities where you feel centered. Remember, being centered means to belong and to be seen, heard, known, and celebrated. **What are the conditions that make you feel centered in this place? What do these conditions teach about inclusion work?**

### From Margin to Center

bell hooks (1952–2021) was a professor, author, and seminal feminist activist in the United States. You can read more about her biography in Unit 2, Lesson 3 (pp. 33–34). This lesson builds on some of hooks' ideas presented in *Feminist Theory: From Margin to Center* (originally published in 1984).[4] In this important book, hooks criticizes the ways feminist theory often centers the experiences of White middle- and upper-class women and rarely includes the "knowledge and awareness of the lives of women and men who live in the margins" (p. xviii).

hooks argues that the people in the center should move out towards the margins. As hooks notes,

> white women who dominate feminist discourse today rarely question whether or not their perspective on women's reality is true to the lived experiences of women as a collective group. Nor are they aware of the extent to which their perspectives reflect race and class biases.
>
> (p. 3)

Universalizing the experiences of the center negates the complex, full, and layered experiences of those in the margins, often further distancing the center from the margins.

If feminism is a movement "to end sexist oppression" (p. 26), then feminist work requires a deep understanding of multiple systems of oppression, including classism, racism, homophobia, ableism, and all other systems which oppress people. In 2020, Mikki Kendall published a bestselling essay collection titled *Hood Feminism: Notes from the Women That a Movement Forgot*. Using an intersectional approach, Kendall argues that the feminist movement has been too limited in who it includes and what issues "count" under the feminist umbrella. You will study more of Kendall's work in Unit 4, Lesson 2 of this unit. hooks believes that when everyone is included, the feminist movement will be centered on a "liberatory ideology that can be shared with everyone" and where "people on the margins who suffer sexist oppression and other forms of group oppression are understood, addressed, and incorporated" (p. 163).

| Term | Definition |
| --- | --- |
| Radical hope | The intentional practice of embracing possibility as a pathway forward. Radical hope asks participants to imagine that change is possible and to create space for new ideas and solutions, including those that represent a radical departure from the status quo (Fishman-Weaver & Walter, 2022). |

A few years ago, during a presidential campaign, I (Jill) heard a presidential candidate say, "Hope is not a strategy." As I was reflecting on these words, I wrote, "If hope is not a strategy, then I have neither hope nor a strategy." I know, of course, that hope cannot be the only strategy. One cannot just hope for change and then change magically happens. If that were the case, we would not need to fight against gender inequity, racial inequity, or any of the number of inequities that exist in this world. However, I do believe that hope should be the foundation of a strategy for change. There are many emotions that fuel change. Sometimes that emotion is fear. Sometimes it is anger. Sometimes it is joy. Always, I believe, there should be hope. "Hope [is] a universal form of resistant imagination. To hope is to believe that situations, circumstances, and practices can be better" (Fishman-Weaver, 2017, p. 10). As you and your classmates work towards equity and justice, look for spaces to celebrate an expansive belief that things can change for the better and for opportunities for you and your peers to be an integral part of that change.

## Expanding Your Understanding

Education can be a powerful tool to disrupt marginalization and expand our understanding. On the same piece of paper with your circle, write the names of one to three communities, groups, or places that are present in your school and that are on the margins of your own understanding.

- ◆ **How can you learn in a humanizing way?**
    - – Remember the conditions that make you feel seen, heard, and celebrated.
    - – Consider learning resources you could reference such as books, documentaries, and podcasts.
    - – Identify gatekeepers, friends, or connections you have who are members of these groups and communities.

## Closing Thoughts

Several years after hooks wrote *Feminist Theory: From Center to Margin*, she published an article called "Choosing the Margin as a Space of Radical Openness" (1989). In this article, she stated that while marginality is a space "imposed by oppressive structures," it can also be a "site of resistance—a location of radical openness and possibility" (p. 23).

- ◆ In this lesson, what have you learned about center and margins?
- ◆ What have you learned about yourself and your peers?
- ◆ How will you commit to radical openness and possibility? Be specific.

Complete the following sentences starters and then share your answers with your peers:

- ◆ Hope is _____.
- ◆ Our change movements need hope because _____.

## Lesson 2: Systems of Oppression—*Outsider Within*

In her poem "Quilting the Black-Eyed Pea (We're Going to Mars)" U.S. poet and activist Nikki Giovanni stated: "The trip to Mars can only be understood through Black Americans" (lines 73–74).[5] Sit with that idea for a moment.

- ◆ What evidence might support such a claim?
- ◆ What does this idea have to do with justice?
- ◆ On whose wisdom do we draw as we journey forward?

In this lesson, you will learn more about intersectionality. While you have encountered this term throughout our studies, the following activities give you an opportunity to go deeper with your learning about this foundational concept.

| INTERSECTIONALITY | | |
|---|---|---|
| **A framework for understanding how multiple identities and *systems of oppressions* intersect to create specific experiences and conditions within systems.** | | |
| **KEY POINT 1—Our experiences happen within systems of advantage (power and privilege) and disadvantage (discrimination and oppression).** | **KEY POINT 2— Experiences and identities are overlapping.** | **KEY POINT 3— Stories are sites of knowledge.** |
| The ways institutions, structures, and norms reinforce discrimination, including but not limited to sexism, racism, classism, heterosexism, ableism, and ageism is called the *system of oppression* (or *matrix of domination*). Systems of oppression are socially and historically specific and connected to power. Patricia Hill Collins is a leading thought leader in this area. | An intersectional approach centers the experiences and "voices of those experiencing overlapping, concurrent forms of oppression in order to understand the depths of the inequalities and the relationships among them in any given context" (UN Women, 2020, para 5). | Intersectional approaches believe that first-person experiences and stories, particularly of individuals from historically marginalized and multiply marginalized backgrounds, are important sites for knowledge. |

## *Outsider Within*—Patricia Hill Collins

Dr. Patricia Hill Collins (1948–) is an American social theorist whose work focuses on race, class, gender, and sexuality. While we have all had outsider experiences, Collins' (1986) *outsider within* standpoint refers to the specific racialized and gendered context that Black women navigate in society. This context matters. Black feminisms center the specific and collective voices and experiences of Black women. Dr. Collins' book *Black Feminist Thought: Knowledge, Consciousness, and the Politics of Empowerment* (first published in 1990) is a leading work on systems of oppression and the intersection of social, racial, and gender justice.

## Black Feminist Thought—*The Combahee River Collective Statement*

Formed in 1974, The Combahee River Collective aimed to create a space and agenda where the voices and experiences of Black women lesbians were included and centered in the work for justice. In a time in U.S. history known for civil rights and women's rights work (1960–1970s), this particular group was often excluded from justice movements. Mainstream feminism often left out people of color, and the national liberation movements for racial justice often excluded women. The Combahee River Collective Statement published in 1977 is a seminal piece of feminist history in the United States, often cited as critical reading on Black feminism, intersectionality, and identity politics.

### On Whose Shoulders?

The name *Combahee River* refers to a Union Army raid led by Harriet Tubman. Harriet Tubman, known as the "Moses of her people," is considered the first African American woman to serve in the military. A formerly enslaved person herself, Tubman dedicated her life to helping enslaved people gain their freedom. During the Combahee River raid, which Tubman helped lead, 750 enslaved people in South Carolina were liberated. In addition to honoring Harriet Tubman, feminists in the Combahee River Collective say the name serves as a reminder that liberation requires political action (Taylor, 2020).

Jigsaw Analysis—In this activity, scholars will work in teams of three or six to analyze excerpts from the Combahee River Collective Statement (1977), connecting them to key concepts from Dr. Patricia Hill Collins' *Outsider Within* (1986) article and their own experiences.

**Jigsaw Steps**

First—Using the reflective questions below, work independently to analyze one of the excerpts below.

Next—In groups, share your responses to the questions and reactions to each excerpt.

Finally—Respond to this prompt: How are systems of oppression present in your community, and what are some ways you and your peers can disrupt these patterns of injustice?

**Primary Source Jigsaw Analysis—Black Feminisms, United States (1970–1980s)**

**Excerpt from the *Combahee River Collective Statement* (1977) republished in *This Bridge Called My Back: Writings by Radical Women of Color* (2015)**

| Excerpt | Key Concept | Text from the Combahee River Collective Statement |
|---|---|---|
| A | Our experiences happen within systems of advantage (power and privilege) and disadvantage (discrimination and oppression). | The most general statement of our politics at the present time would be that we are actively committed to struggling against racial, sexual, heterosexual, and class oppression, and see as our particular task the development of integrated analysis and practice based upon the fact that the major systems of oppression are interlocking. The synthesis of these oppressions creates the conditions of our lives. As Black women we see Black feminism as the logical political movement to combat the manifold and simultaneous oppressions that all women of color face (p. 210). |
| B | Experiences and identities are overlapping. | A political contribution which we feel we have already made is the expansion of the feminist principle that the personal is political. In our consciousness-raising sessions, for example, we have in many ways gone beyond white women's revelations because we are dealing with the implications of race and class as well as sex (p. 213). |

| Excerpt | Key Concept | Text from the Combahee River Collective Statement |
|---------|-------------|----------------------------------------------------|
| C | Stories are sites of knowledge. | Above all else, our politics initially sprang from the shared belief that Black women are inherently valuable, that our liberation is a necessity not as an adjunct to somebody else's because of our need as human persons for autonomy. This may seem so obvious as to sound simplistic, but it is apparent that no other ostensibly progressive movement has ever considered our specific oppression as a priority or worked seriously for the ending of that oppression (p. 212). |

*Concepts from P.H. Collins,* Outsider Within *(1986)*

## Reflective Questions

- ◆ Summarize your excerpt in your own words. What is the key message?
- ◆ Connect this excerpt to one of the key terms of vocabulary from our WGST lessons.
- ◆ Connect this excerpt to a specific historical event or person's work.
- ◆ Connect this excerpt to your own lives and community. How does this message relate to something you have experienced or witnessed in your community or the news?
- ◆ What are your reactions to this statement? What do you agree with? What would you challenge? Are there any points you would like to qualify with more information?

**Exit Question:** How are systems of oppression present in your community, and what are some ways you and your peers can disrupt these patterns of injustice?

## Lesson 3: Mother Earth—Gendered Impacts of Climate Change

I want to live on a planet that can hold us. I believe we can all still help it, us, do so. If nothing else, why not try? Why not hope, and then act as if? This is our one wild, lone home; what other choice do we have?

(Kwan, 2021)

| Term | Definition |
| --- | --- |
| Climate justice | A movement that acknowledges how climate change affects people in marginalized communities in disproportional and exponential ways. This movement then advocates for these inequalities to be addressed and for solutions to be implemented. |
| Sustainable Development Goal (SDG) 13 | The United Nations' SDG 13 is "Take urgent action to combat climate change and its impacts." This is an urgent call because the consequences of climate change will only increase its destruction of our world, its land, its water, and its people, particularly those most vulnerable. |
| Intersectional environmentalism and intersectional environmental justice | *Intersectional environmentalism* is a term coined by Leah Thomas, an "eco-communicator, aka an environmentalist with a love for writing + creativity" (Thomas, n.d.). She defines *intersectional environmentalism* as<br><br>An inclusive version of environmentalism that advocates for both the protection of people and the planet [and] acknowledges the overlap between systemic harm against Black, Indigenous, and people of color (BIPOC) communities and the Earth. The movement also recognizes the disproportional effects of climate change on other marginalized groups, including people with disabilities as well as women and gender minorities.<br>(Capshaw-Mack, 2021) |

"Climate change refers to long-term shifts in temperatures and weather patterns. . . .Since the 1800s, human activities have been the main driver of climate change" (United Nations, n.d.-d). The decade 2011–2020 was the warmest decade ever recorded, and the "consequences of climate change now include, among others, intense droughts, water scarcity, severe fires, rising sea levels, flooding, melting polar ice, catastrophic storms, and declining biodiversity" (United Nations, n.d.-d). As Ayana Elizabeth Johnson and Katharine K. Wilkinson note in their climate anthology *All We Can Save: Truth, Courage, and Solutions for the Climate Crisis*, "The climate crisis is not gender neutral." It is, instead, "a powerful 'threat multiplier,' making existing vulnerabilities and injustices worse" (2021, p. xviii). Because of climate change, women and girls are disproportionately in danger of dying, falling into poverty, being displaced from their homes, being forced into early marriage, and becoming victims of gender-based violence (Johnson & Wilkinson, 2021, p. xviii).

In many cultures where women and girls are responsible for collecting water, growing food, and gathering wood, the effects of climate change make these tasks more burdensome and dangerous (Johnson & Wilkinson, 2021, p. xviii). Climate change has a particularly devastating effect on women of color; therefore, some environmentalists are utilizing an intersectional approach to analyze and take action to address the overlapping injustices and challenges compounded by racism, sexism, and the climate crisis. The disproportional effects of climate change on marginalized groups include lack of access to clean air and water and exposure to toxic waste and hazardous air.

## Young People at the Forefront of Climate Justice

Katharine Wilkinson asks, "What are your superpowers, and how can those be contributed in some way to the work that needs doing on climate" (Johnson & Wilkinson, 2021)?

Many women and girls who are disproportionately affected by climate change are also leading the way to combat climate change. In this lesson, you will learn about important young people who are leading the way toward climate justice. As you read these stories, use the graphic organizer below to keep track of the strengths (superpowers), actions, and connections you can make to take action yourself.

### Greta Thunberg, Sweden

Greta Thunberg is a climate activist from Sweden who first learned about the earth's climate crisis when she was eight years old. Since then, she has devoted her life to climate advocacy work. She began a youth protest movement by striking against climate change. This movement eventually led to *Fridays for Future*, where an international group of students strike on Fridays to challenge government officials to (1) create policies to prevent climate change and (2) to demand that fossil fuel industries switch over to renewable energy. Thunberg has addressed world leaders multiple times and challenged them to address the climate crisis with urgency and action. Her words "You are never too small to make a difference" (UN Climate Change, 2018, 0:32) inspired youth all over the world that they could use their voices and their actions to be an impetus for change. In 2022, Thunberg published a handbook called *The Climate Book* with "contributions from more than 100 academics, thinkers and campaigners . . . to help readers connect the dots between threats to the climate environment, sustainability and indigenous populations—among others—and is intended as a guide to understanding and activism" (Lawless, 2022). Thunberg has received worldwide attention for her advocacy work, including being named the youngest *Time* Person of Year and being nominated for the Nobel Peace Prize in 2019, 2020, and 2021.

### Leah Namugerwa, Uganda

Uganda has a tropical climate, and climate change has disrupted the rainy season causing harsh droughts and other natural disasters. Flooding, landslides, heat waves, and extreme drought have killed people; displaced them; and disrupted water and food supplies, employment, and infrastructure. These effects of climate change have disproportionally affected women, as women are less likely to own land, have access to literacy education, and have the legal authority to make decisions that affect their safety and security (Acosta et al., 2015).

Leah Namugerwa first became a climate activist in 2018 after hearing about Greta Thunberg. When her father told her that Greta Thunberg was not much older than she was, Namugerwa decided that she could fight climate change, too. She began striking on Fridays and joined *Fridays for Future* (Earthday.org, 2019). She continues to strike and has expanded her activism to create a petition to ban plastic bag use in Uganda. When she realized that deforestation was causing landslides in Uganda, she created *Birthday Trees*, a program that encourages planting trees instead of spending money on birthday parties (*Leah Namugerwa*, n.d.). For her 15th birthday, Namugerwa planted 200 trees; for her 16th birthday, she planted 500 trees; and for her 17th birthday, Namugerwa and her friends planted 700 trees. Her goal is that her program will inspire the planting of one million trees (UNA-UK, 2021).

### Jamie Margolin: Seattle, Washington, United States

Jamie Margolin, a teenager from Seattle, Washington, was inspired to fight climate change after learning about the Indigenous young people who protested against the Dakota Access Pipeline at Standing Rock. Margolin watched the devastating effects of Hurricane Maria in Puerto Rico and then experienced difficulty breathing after smoke from Canadian wildfires blanketed Seattle. She organized *Zero Hour*, an intersectional climate action movement that within a year grew from a group of her friends to a national event. Zero Hour's mission is to "center the voices of diverse youth in the conversation around climate and environmental justice" (*Zero Hour*, n.d.). While Zero Hour advocates for policies that directly affect the climate, such as educating people on the Green New Deal, they also focus on how oppressive systems such as racism, colonialism, and sexism intersect with climate change (*Zero Hour: Our Actions*, n.d.). Margolin said,

> You just look to see who is being hit hardest by unnatural disasters, as I call them. It's easy to pinpoint: everyone who is the victim of a system of oppression—colonialism or racism, anyone who is poor. The people who are held down by systems of oppression in our society are the same people most vulnerable to the climate crisis.
>
> (Jacques, 2019)

Her goal is to run for Congress so that she can bring her ideals and ideas to government.

### Isra Hirsi: Minneapolis, Minnesota, United States

Before Isra Hirsi even knew what an activist was, she knew that she wanted to change the world. As the daughter of Congresswoman Ilhan Omar, she grew up participating in protests and thinking about change movements. When she was a first-year high school student, she joined her school's environmentalism club and other social justice groups. She found that although these groups were addressing important issues there was very limited diversity of voices and perspectives in the school groups. At school, the groups she participated in addressed the Minnesota pipeline going through Indigenous treaty lands and the ways children of color were affected by poor air and water quality. Hirsi wanted to expand this important conversation by intentionally bringing more diverse voices and perspectives to solve these challenges. Therefore, Isra Hirsi co-founded *US Youth Climate Strike*, a movement that works with youth organizers who are committed to climate justice across the United States. US Youth Climate Strike brings to light the ways that climate change affects people of color and those in low-income communities in more potentially devastating ways. It is focused on how climate justice and racial justice intersect, noting that "the climate movement needs a drastic change toward diversity before we can truly be intersectional and effective" (Kelly, 2020).

### Xiye Bastida: Atlacomulco, Mexico, and New York City, United States

Xiye Bastida, whose name means "soft rain," is a Mexican-Chilean climate activist who is a member of the Oltomi Toltec Nation, an Indigenous nation in Mexico. Bastida became passionate about climate change after she experienced how extreme weather disproportionally affects smaller, Indigenous communities. Although Indigenous populations make up just five percent of the global population, their lands are home to 80% of the earth's biodiversity. Indigenous people are often marginalized and discriminated against, and the lands they call home are often destroyed and polluted. Bastida and her family were forced to flee their home after an extreme drought followed by continuous rain caused flooding in her hometown of San Pedro Tultepec, a town outside of Mexico City. She and her family moved to New York City, where she joined an environmentalist club at school. Bastida began advocating for climate justice and Indigenous rights. In 2019, she helped organize a climate strike at her school, which 600 students participated in. Bastida speaks on climate justice as a leader in the youth climate strike movement Fridays for Future. She also approaches the climate crisis from a space of radical hope. She "understands that the climate crisis is getting worse everyday, but chooses hope and action over despair" (Zoeller, 2021).

# Youth Activists at the Forefront of Climate Justice

Name _____ Date_____

## Part I—Changemaker Profiles

| Activist | Greatest Strength (Superpower) | Summary (Actions, Interesting Facts) | Connection (What can you do with this story?) |
|---|---|---|---|
| Greta Thunberg | | | |
| Leah Namugerwa | | | |
| Jamie Margolin | | | |
| Isra Hirsi | | | |
| Xiye Bastida | | | |

## Part I—Taking Action

Each of the youth activists highlighted in this lesson began their work after noticing how climate change affected local communities. **How is climate change affecting people in your community, particularly people from marginalized communities?** Research the answer to this question and create a plan for how you and your peers can advance intersectional climate justice in your local community.

| Team Names | Greatest Strengths (Superpower) | Local Issues | Plan to Take Action |
|---|---|---|---|
| | | | |

## Unit 4—The Personal Is Political: The Power of More Complete Stories

In Concept 1, you reviewed Carol Hanisch's seminal feminist phrase "the personal is political" (1970). This unit builds on that concept.

Your lived experiences, identities, and culture help shape how you understand and view the world. Your lived experiences also give you insight and humanity. Much like perception and knowledge, your experiences are fluid and overlapping. The relationships you have, places you call home, and lessons you learn influence your constantly evolving understanding of the world. Your lived experiences are also informed by the people you love, the places where you find beauty, the media you consume, and the music in your head.

Additionally, your experiences are influenced by the policies, practices, and institutions with which you interact. The narrative you are living is informed by complex systems of oppression, privilege, and discrimination, which may be raced, classed, and gendered.

In this book, we (Kathryn and Jill) operate from a working hypothesis that the more we can learn about each other's experiences, identities, and perspectives, the more whole the world becomes. In Hebrew, the phrase *Tikkun Olam* translates roughly to working to heal, repair, and transform the world. This work of making the world whole, of repair and renewal, requires clear vision, empathy, and a willingness to admit to places where your own perspective was too limited or narrow. It also requires action and a willingness to change.

Through this learning, this openness, this making whole, you have the opportunity to reimagine broken systems, repair strained relationships, and join in a collective narrative pointed toward equity and justice. In the following unit, you will bring theory to action by organizing initiatives and engaging in research to address food insecurity and access to health care (including mental health) in your local communities.

### Key Term: *Solidarity*

Solidarity, rooted in justice, is about acting with unity to support marginalized groups. Solidarity is not about the person who is doing the acting but about the beliefs on which they are acting. Solidarity requires putting your own comfort, power, and sense of belonging at risk. Practicing solidarity requires acting out of principle, even when the outcome may make your life harder (or less comfortable).

◆ *Performative allyship* is when someone does something they think is "good" (and often quite safe) and then brags about or posts photographs of what a great job or important work they have done advocating on behalf of someone with less privilege. This is both damaging and othering to marginalized groups. Those working in solidarity do not act for credit or accolades.

I (Kathryn) like to think of solidarity as acting on the core belief that we belong to each other.

### Related Term: *Upstander*

In schools, *upstanders* are an example of people who act in solidarity. An upstander intervenes when someone (or group) is being bullied. They are not passive like the bystander who merely observes the bullying. Instead, they take it upon themselves to work from whatever influence they do have to stop the injustice. They don't do this for their own gain; they do it because they believe their actions will reduce harm and oppression.

## Lesson 1: Chimamanda Ngozi Adichie—"The Danger of a Single Story"

**Teaching Note**

This lesson can be a powerful community-building activity. It also requires clear norms and a culture of courage. Before asking students to write and share the Take a Reflective Beat activity, spend some time creating (or reviewing) clear norms and discussing courage, empathy, and vulnerability.

### How You See Me—An Activity on Perspective

Part I: In a word or short phrase, how would the following people describe you?

| | |
|---|---|
| ◆ Someone who first meets you <br> ◆ A teacher <br> ◆ Someone who participates in a group activity with you <br> ◆ A new friend | ◆ Someone you have known for a long time <br> ◆ Your best friend (or a very good friend) <br> ◆ A close family member <br> ◆ Yourself |

Part II: Think about the different ways people see and know you.

- ◆ How do you feel about the way these people in your life might describe you?
- ◆ Who do you think would describe you most accurately? Least accurately?
- ◆ Are you frustrated with any of the descriptions other people might have of you? If so, why?

People are complicated, complex, and multifaceted. The single words or phrases you wrote in the exercise above are incomplete; so, too, are single stories. When all you see in someone is a single story, you miss the complicated, complex, and multifaceted layers. You miss their complete story. Complete stories are often challenging; however, they are also a bridge to empathy. Empathy, according to the American Psychological Association, is "understanding a person from [their] frame of reference rather than one's own, or vicariously experiencing that person's feelings, perceptions, and thoughts" (*APA Dictionary of Psychology*, n.d.). Empathy requires us to move past single stories, to listen actively, and to engage in perspective sharing.

### Chimamanda Ngozi Adichie—"The Danger of a Single Story"

Chimamanda Ngozi Adichie is an award-winning Nigerian author whose TED Talk, "The Danger of a Single Story" (2009), is one of the most watched TED Talks of all time (with over 30 million views).

Watch Adichie's TED Talk, "The Danger of a Single Story," and then discuss the following questions with your peers.

- Adichie said this in her talk: "I've always felt that it is impossible to engage properly with a place or a person without engaging with all of the stories of that place and that person. The consequence of the single story is this: It robs people of dignity" (2009, 13:37). What are other consequences of the single story?
- Adichie stated, "Stories matter. Many stories matter. Stories have been used to dispossess and to malign, but stories can also be used to empower and to humanize. Stories can break the dignity of people, but stories can also repair that broken dignity" (2009, 17:28). What are some examples of ways that stories can empower, humanize, and repair broken dignity?
- How do single stories relate to our conversations around gender? Consider gender roles, stereotypes, relationships, societal structures, media, and ideas about masculinity and femininity. How do these single stories impact how society is structured, our relationships with one another, and our personal identities?
- How can we change these single stories?

### Take a Reflective Beat

Adichie said,

> The Palestinian poet Mourid Barghouti writes that if you want to dispossess a people, the simplest way to do it is to tell their story and to start with, "secondly." Start the story with the arrows of the Native Americans, and not with the arrival of the British, and you have an entirely different story. Start the story with the failure of the African state, and not with the colonial creation of the African state, and you have an entirely different story.
>
> (2009, 10:04)

In your journal, write down some ideas about what single stories you feel others believe about you. Then, as a poem, paragraph, or list, challenge or complicate those perceptions by answering this prompt:

> The first thing you need to know is . . .

This exercise may have brought up some big feelings. It is difficult to be misunderstood, when other people's stories of us start with "Secondly . . ." instead of "The first thing you need to know. . . ." If you feel comfortable, share your thoughts on this exercise with your peers. As others are sharing, remember that they, too, may be sharing something vulnerable. Listen in a way that can build a bridge toward empathy.

## Reflect on It

◆ How do things change when "the first thing you need to know" is left out of your story?
◆ How has your knowledge of your peers expanded in this lesson?
◆ What are some ways you can connect to people with empathy so that you learn a more complete version of their story?

**Lesson 2—Food Insecurity: Why Hunger Is an Intersectional and Feminist Issue**

 Thought Questions
- ◆ What do you think "food insecurity" means?
- ◆ Why is food insecurity a feminist issue?

| Term | Definition |
|------|------------|
| Food insecurity | Defined by the Food and Agriculture Organization of the United Nations as "lack[ing] regular access to enough safe and nutritious food for normal growth and development and an active and healthy life." Food insecurity ranges from mild to severe, from unreliable access to food, to reduced quality and variety of food, to reduced quantity of food (including skipping meals), to not eating for a day or more (Food and Agriculture Organization of the United Nations, n.d.). Food insecurity is more likely to affect women than men and is also mostly likely to affect women and children of color. |
| Food justice | A direct response to combatting food insecurity, particularly for those in marginalized communities. Individuals involved in the food justice movement seek to eliminate food insecurity by addressing food insecurity from a gendered, economic, racial, and political standpoint. |

**Just Like Feminism, Fighting Food Insecurity Is for Everybody**

According to the United Nations World Food Program, "Of the 811 million people who are food insecure in the world right now, nearly 60 percent are women and girls" (n.d.-b). In low-income countries, women constitute nearly half of the agricultural workforce. However, despite their contribution to food production and meal preparation, because of gender inequity they often "eat least, last and least well." Since women are more often caregivers, they are also more likely to share their portion of food with children, and the cumulative effects of hunger can result in malnutrition and illness (Oxfam, 2019, p. 8). As Vandana Shiva (2009) stated in her article "Women and the Gendered Politics of Food," "From seed to table, the food chain is gendered" (p. 17).

The United Nations' SDG 2 is to "End hunger, achieve food security and improved nutrition and promote sustainable agriculture" (n.d.). To help meet the target of SDG 2, the UN World Food Programme, which was awarded the Nobel Peace Prize in 2020, is committed to ending both food insecurity and hunger. Much of their work includes striving to increase gender equality so that women and girls have the tools and resources to feed themselves and their families. Many other organizations and people are working to accomplish this goal, as well.

---

 **Thought Question**

◆ What organizations are addressing food insecurity in your own community?

---

Food insecurity is a global challenge across low-, middle-, and high-income countries. For example, in the United States, 11.1% of households are food insecure. However, according to the U.S. Department of Agriculture, the rates are 30.3% for households with a single mother and 14.7% for women who live alone. Unfortunately, food insecurity is often overlooked and misunderstood. In the United States, many "treat hunger as a moral failing" (Kendall, 2020, p. 32) instead of "an indictment of our society" (Kendall, 2020, p. 42).

### Responding to "Hunger" Mikki Kendall—*Hood Feminism*

Mikki Kendall (1976–) is an author and an activist whose book *Hood Feminism: Notes from the Women That the Movement Forgot* is an indictment of how the feminist movement, despite claiming to represent everyone, has alienated women in marginalized communities, particularly in communities of color. Building on Crenshaw's work on intersectionality (see Concept 2), Kendall challenges that for the feminist movement to be a movement for all, it must prioritize eliminating racism and commit to affirming and expanding access to basic human needs, including wage justice, adequate housing and transportation, quality medical care, and food security. This social justice work is inherently intersectional.

Read and respond to the quotes below from Kendall's "Hunger" chapter in *Hood Feminism*.

> We know in the abstract that poverty is a feminist issue. Indeed, we think of it as a feminist issue *for other countries*, and that we are in a place where bootstraps and grit can be enough to get anyone who wants it bad enough out of poverty. But the reality is that it takes a lot more than gumption.
>
> (Kendall, 2020, p. 31)

◆ In your own words, what is this quote saying?
◆ How does this quote relate to our earlier lessons on *global feminisms* and *intersectionality*?
◆ Defend, refute, or qualify "poverty is a feminist issue." What does this look like in your local community?

As a society, we tend to treat hunger as a moral failing, as a sign that someone is lacking in a fundamental way. We remember to combat hunger around the holidays, but we judge the mothers who have to rely on food banks, free or reduced lunches at school, or food stamps for not being able to stand against a problem that baffles governments around the world. Indeed, we treat poverty itself like a crime, like the women experiencing it are making bad choices for themselves and their children on purpose. We ignore that they don't have a good choice available.

(Kendall, 2020, p. 32–33)

◆ In your own words, what is this quote saying?
◆ What emotions does this quote bring up for you?
◆ Defend, refute, or qualify—"As a society, we tend to treat hunger as a moral failing."
◆ What are the consequences of living in a society that treats poverty like a crime?

Why is it that we're more inclined to create programs to combat obesity than ones that meaningfully address hunger? . . . Politicians use fatphobia and make obesity a scapegoat to deflect attention away from the policies that have adversely affected the health of low-income communities.

(Kendall, 2020, p. 37–38)

◆ In your own words, what is this quote is saying?
◆ As Kendall asks, "Why is it that we're more inclined to create programs to combat obesity than ones that meaningfully address hunger?"
◆ How might policies that claim their aim is to combat obesity actually distract from the greater justice issues of health disparities in low-income communities?

Feminism has to come through to combat food insecurity from higher prices for fresh foods to insufficient government funding for programs that address hunger on a systemic level. Without support from feminists with privilege and access, families facing food insecurity will suffer despite their best efforts. Hunger saps your energy, your will; it eats up the space that you might have used to achieve with the need to survive. As feminist issues go, there are none that span more women and their families than this one.

(Kendall, 2020, p. 45)

- ◆ In your own words, what is this quote saying?
- ◆ What would it look like to address food insecurity on a systemic level?
- ◆ Defend, refute, or qualify—"As feminist issues go, there are none that span more women and their families than this one."

## Food Insecurity for Women of Color and the COVID Pandemic

The COVID global pandemic is "a pandemic on top of a pandemic" (World Food Program USA, n.d.-a). "Nearly 2.37 billion people (or 30% of the global population) lacked access to adequate food in 2020—a rise of 320 million in just one year" (The World Bank, n.d.). The causes of this increase in hunger include disrupted supply chains, increased food prices, job losses, and missed school meals. While these disruptions are harmful to women everywhere, they are further compounded in lower income countries and in communities of color. The U.S. Census Bureau took a House Pulse Survey the week of August 19–31, 2020. When compared with other racial and gender groups that week, significantly more Latina and Black women reported that they lost income and did not have enough food (Tucker & Ewing-Nelson, 2020). These statistics do not include all groups in the United States; in particular, undocumented immigrants and resettled refugees are often missing from these reports. As with other social issues we have explored through these lessons, historically and continuously marginalized and multiply marginalized groups are most affected by food insecurity.

## Exit Slip

Kendall stated, "You can't be a feminist who ignores hunger" (2020, p. 37). Defend, refute, or qualify this statement and then give examples of the relationship between hunger and equity.

## Lesson 3: Praxis, Food Insecurity—A Local Justice Issue

| Term | Definition |
|------|------------|
| Praxis | The intersection of action and theory. It is where you take what you learn and turn it into action. |

In the next activity, you will engage in praxis as you take a deep dive into what food insecurity means for your local community. This work includes *asset mapping* (Simmons, 2012) by looking at the organizations and individuals engaged in justice and advocacy work and then developing and implementing a plan to support these efforts.

As you have learned throughout these units, food insecurity is pervasive. If this issue is personal to you—if you and your family experience or have experienced food insecurity—know that you are not alone. Prior to the pandemic, 20.1 million youth received free lunches, and 1.7 million youth received reduced-price lunches (School Nutrition Association, n.d.). These statistics, like all statistics, do not tell a full story of food security for youth in the United States. For example, not all youth who qualify for free and reduced-price lunches are experiencing food insecurity. Further, many youth and families who are struggling with food insecurity may not qualify for this program, may not know how to access it, or may choose not to participate. My (Kathryn's) childhood lived experiences included several of these situations.

If you and your family are struggling with access to food, groceries, or other resources and no one at your school is aware, please talk with your teacher, school counselor, or other trusted adult. These professionals may be able to connect you and your family with supports. Last semester, I (Kathryn) met with a student who told me about a time when his school lunch account had gone into a negative balance. After a couple weeks, the cafeteria worker told him that unless his family put more money in the account she wouldn't be able to serve him any longer. He went to the office staff to ask if his family could have an extension on adding money to the account. It had been a tough several years for his family. The office staff gave him a form to take home. His family filled out the form, and he didn't have to pay for lunch again. He also started receiving a weekend snack pack that he could share with his siblings. His family didn't know about these supports until he brought that form home. This same young man graduates college this year and is becoming a high school teacher. He told me that he wants to make sure all his students know about these and other resources that help thread care to families who are doing the best they can.

Your lived experiences matter. Your lived experiences also belong to you. As we engage in group work related to food insecurity in your community, it is your choice about how much, how little, with whom, and when you share (or don't share) key parts of your story with your peers.

Name _____  Date _____

## Food Insecurity in My Community—Praxis Project

| RESEARCH | BARRIERS | RESOURCES | ACTION |
|---|---|---|---|
| What are the barriers to and scope of food insecurity in your community (school, city, or state)?<br><br>*Consider high food prices, lack of access to grocery stores and fresh food, poverty, climate change, supply issues, gender discrimination, and underemployment.* | How do other systems of injustice influence this issue?<br><br>*Consider racism, sexism, ageism, and ableism.* Note: you may need to seek out disaggregated data (see p. 148) to better answer this question. | Name specific organizations and individuals who are engaged in work to reduce food insecurity and increase food justice in your community.*<br><br>*Consider food banks, food pantries, soup kitchens, homeless shelters, community gardens, warming shelters, and safe houses and women's shelters.* | How will you join these efforts? Write a specific plan below and then carry out that plan.<br><br>*Consider serving at one of the organizations you researched, organizing a food drive, delivering meals to veterans or older adults.*** |
| | | | |

**References:** Where did you go for information on this project? In addition to website and reference materials, also cite organizations and individuals who informed your work on this project.

\* This work is aligned to our work around *radical hope* (see p. 74) and *asset-based approaches* (see p. 22).
\*\* Effective involvement is *ongoing* and *rooted in justice*.

---

**Lesson 4: Beverly Greene, Psychological Resistance**

 **Thought Questions**

- ◆ Have you ever felt like a doctor or counselor wasn't hearing you? What factors contributed to this communication challenge?
- ◆ How are mental health and social justice work connected?

---

| Term | Definition |
|---|---|
| Heterosexism | Excluding or omitting the perspectives, experiences, cultures, and histories of gay and queer people and casting heterosexuality and heterosexual relationships as the norm. |
| Eurocentrism | Excluding or omitting the multiple global perspectives, experiences, cultures, and histories that make our world and casting European culture and history as the norm. |

## Dr. Beverly Greene—Intersectional Psychology

Dr. Beverly Greene's (1950–) work explores best practices and care for people who are *multiply marginalized*. Greene specializes in the psychology of women with an emphasis on gender and racial issues. How do different aspects of a person's identity, including their experiences with sexism, heterosexism, and racism, influence their privilege, oppression, and overall mental health? This is one of the guiding questions that led Greene to introduce *intersectional psychology* to her field.

Greene's landmark article (1986) "When the Therapist is White and the Patient is Black: Considerations for Psychotherapy in the Feminist Heterosexual and Lesbian Communities" spotlighted the ways race, gender, and identity can influence the patient-doctor relationship and ultimately care. Psychology, both as a practice and in research, is "not a value-neutral science" (Chewniski, 2010, para 6). Greene stresses that researchers make important decisions about who to include and therefore who is excluded in their studies. Additionally, Greene said that psychology needs to expand its understanding and learn more intentionally from women who live outside the United States. In much the same way that systems of racism, sexism, and classism can create blind spots, a Eurocentric lens may also "obscure our ability to understand their realities and experiences" (Chewniski, 2010, para 7).

This lesson asked you to think about potential challenges in communication with health and mental health professionals. In the next activity, you and your peers will consider the relationship between mental health, social justice, and feminism as you develop an inclusive and intersectional protocol for care.

# Intersectional Protocol for Care

Name _____ Date_____

**Directions:** Using an intersectional approach, organize a group research project on a mental or physical health topic that matters to you and your peers. Choosing a research topic requires reflection, information gathering, and synthesis. As a team, use the following protocol to identify your research topic and draft your research questions.

---

**Thematic Brainstorm**

**Themes: Mental Health, Physical Health, Social Justice, Youth, and Feminism**

Working in teams, explore the relationship among these five themes.

- ◆ How are two or more of these themes connected to our WGST studies?
- ◆ How are two or more themes connected to your own lives?

**Starter Questions**

- ◆ How is youth health a social justice issue?
  - – Consider gender justice.
  - – Consider racial justice.
  - – Consider access, especially for youth.

- ◆ How could an intersectional perspective improve health or mental health outcomes?
- ◆ Who are the most important allies and advocates you know for health or mental health?

---

**Professionals**

Identify a health or mental health care professional in your local or school community.

- ◆ Examples include a school nurse, school counselor, school psychologist, pediatrician, or community health care worker.

---

| Wisdom to Share | Wisdom to Learn |
|---|---|
| What have you learned in this class or your own research about physical health, mental health, intersectionality, and/or feminism that you would like to share with this professional? | What questions do you have about physical health, mental health, intersectionality, and/or feminism that you would like to ask this professional? |
| ✎ | ✎ |

**Research Questions**

*Review your notes so far. As a team, select a focus area for further research.*

Once you have selected a focus area, write three open-ended research questions.

✎ _____

_____

✎ _____

_____

✎ _____

_____

Final projects can be presented in a research paper, Google Slides presentation, or video. All presentations should include the following:

- ◆ thesis statement,
- ◆ three research questions and completed answers to those questions,
- ◆ interview with at least one community professional,
- ◆ references to at least three key terms or figures from our WGST lessons connecting them to your research,
- ◆ references to at least three additional resources your team has identified,
- ◆ a clear statement on why intersectionality matters to your topic or focus area, and
- ◆ a call to action or justice

# Concept Synthesis Project: Radical Hope and Intersectionality—Collage Compare and Contrast

Name _____ Date_____

## Part I—Research Collage

Our last two units have focused on *intersectionality*. In these lessons, you have met scholars, psychologists, authors, activists, and teachers engaged in powerful justice work. **Select one of the key figures** introduced in these lessons and answer the questions. Go beyond our lessons and learn through additional research!

| Chimamanda Ngozi Adichie Dr. Beverly Greene Dr. Patricia Hill Collins | bell hooks Alice Walker Leah Namugerwa | Jamie Margolin Isra Hirsi Xiye Bastida |
|---|---|---|

- ◆ Create a list of their identities.

  *Consider race, ethnicity, national origin, age, gender, faith/religious affiliation, home language, (dis)ability, and others.*

- ◆ Create a list of the different social groups to which they belong(ed).

  *Consider family, friends/peers, sports and activities, faith communities, neighborhoods, and others.*

- ◆ Consider other key identity markers that represent their strengths and works.

  *What can you learn about them personally and professionally?*

- ◆ Gather photographs, artifacts, and magazine or newspaper clippings that illustrate key items from each of the three categories listed above.
- ◆ Get creative! Collage your materials into a portrait. You may interpret "portrait" as literally or abstractly as you like.

## Reflective Questions

- ◆ What surprised you in creating this new research collage? Reread the earlier definition of intersectionality. How do the identities and experiences in this collage work in concert or conflict with each other?
- ◆ What role does or did power and agency play in the work, identities, and experiences of your key figure?

- What identities were easiest to find information about? Which identities were hardest to find information about? Why do you think that is?
- What aspects of your key figure's identity, experiences, and work did you choose to celebrate and why?
- Where can you find examples of representation, resistance, or radical hope in your research collage?

## Part II: Identity Collage

Building on these units' focus on intersectionality, this synthesis project celebrates the ways your first-person experiences, cultures, identities, and backgrounds as important sites for knowledge is inherent to intersectional approaches.

### Guiding Questions

- What can you learn from exploring a more complete personal history?
- How can an intersectional understanding support justice work?

Through this activity, you will have the opportunity to reflect on your multiple identities, strengths, and talents and the way your story can inspire you to engage in justice work.

## Directions

- Create a list of your identities.

  *Consider race, ethnicity, national origin, age, gender, faith/religious affiliation, home language, (dis)ability, and others.*

- Create a list of the different social groups to which you belong.

  *Consider family, friends and peers, sports and activities, faith communities, neighborhoods, and others.*

- Consider other key identity markers that represent your strengths and make you you.

  *Consider personal motto, favorite color, strengths and talents, passions, favorite place, favorite food, hobbies, etc.*

- Gather photographs, artifacts, and magazine or newspaper clippings that illustrate key items from each of the three categories listed earlier.

- Get creative! Collage your materials into a self-portrait. You may interpret "self-portrait" as literally or abstractly as you like.

### Reflection Questions

- ◆ What surprised you in creating your identity collage? Reread the definition of intersectionality. How do your identities work in concert or conflict with each other?
- ◆ What role does power play in your personal identities and experiences?
- ◆ What identities are most important to you? What makes these identities important?

### Radical Hope Reflection, Research, and Art Statement

As the final piece of your proseminar project, write a research and artist statement on these two collages. You may present your statement as a paper, an audio recording, or poster.

**Prompt:** *Compare and contrast your research collage and your identity collage. What do you notice that makes you proud? What questions do you still have about identity and intersectionality? In making your collages, what aspects did you choose to celebrate? What are your takeaways from your research, and how will you use these ideas in your life and community?*

**Closing Thought**—Centering radical hope does not ignore or erase discriminatory and problematic practices—conversely, focusing on hope calls these practices out plainly and says that with intentionally we can (and must) do better (Fishman-Weaver, 2017).

### Helpful Links

- ◆ Chimamanda Ngozi Adichie called "The Danger of a Single Story": www.youtube.com/watch?v=D9Ihs241zeg&t=1s
- ◆ "Teaching at the intersections: (Learning for Justice Magazine Article): www.learningforjustice.org/magazine/summer-2016/teaching-at-the-intersections
- ◆ Toolkit for "Teaching at the intersections" (resource list by Learning for Justice broken down by grade bands): www.learningforjustice.org/magazine/summer-2016/toolkit-for-teaching-at-the-intersections
- ◆ Fridays for Future: https://fridaysforfuture.org
- ◆ Youth Direct Action Fund (YDAF): https://strikewithus.org/ydaf
- ◆ Zero Hour: http://thisiszerohour.org
- ◆ Nikki Giovanni, "Quilting the Black-Eyed Pea (We're going to Mars)": www.youtube.com/watch?v=cMKSSlaqTLE

## Extension Exercises for Concept 2

**Making Learning Visible:** These lessons offer many possibilities for sharing work, extending the conversation around intersectionality, and making learning visible. The three activities listed below could all be built out for community-wide showcases.

- ◆ **Intersectional Protocol for Care Presentations**—If scholars complete the research for their intersectional care work, these could be presented at a powerful intersectional health showcase. Invite school nurses, community health workers, counselors, doctors, and mental health professionals to learn with and from the scholar researchers.
- ◆ **Making Connections Collection**—In this activity, scholars research psychologists, authors, activists, and teachers engaged in powerful justice work. Share the findings in presentations for families or reformat this content into a book or presentation suitable for elementary scholars and make this a teaching presentation.
- ◆ **Identity Collage Gallery**—This synthesis activity has potential for an arts-integration or art-collaboration project with the art educators in your building. Scholars can develop their collages into more formal art pieces for an identity gallery. Invite families, educators, peers, administrators, and others from your school community to view these powerful images. Following a gallery walk, scholars can also host dialogues on identity, belonging, and inclusion with these stakeholders.

### Gallery Walk

Do a gallery walk to explore the art exhibition *The Colour of the Climate Crisis*: https://thecolouroftheclimatecrisis.art

## Notes

[1] This is a reference to "The Rose That Grew Out of Concrete," a poem by Tupac Shakur about thriving in places that are inhospitable to growth.

[2] Border-crossing theory explores the physical and ideological borders that separate human experience.

[3] Coverture is an older legal doctrine with roots in English common law. This doctrine made wives subservient to their husband's authority. These laws kept women from owning property or having custody of children in the case of a divorce and offered limited or no protection against domestic abuse.

[4] hooks released subsequent editions of *Feminist Theory: From Margin to Center* in 2000 and 2015.

[5] You can find a link to Giovanni performing this poem in the section appendix.

# Motherland—History, Health, and Policy Change

## Advisory Editor Concept Foreword
## by Dr. Dena Lane-Bonds

**Dr. Dena Lane-Bonds** (she/her) is a postdoctoral research scholar for the Initiative for Race Research and Justice in the Department of Teaching and Learning at Vanderbilt University. She received her PhD in educational leadership and policy analysis from the University of Missouri, where she studied the experiences of graduate students navigating homelessness and housing insecurity. In higher education, her research and efforts have centered on cultivating equitable and inclusive teaching, learning, and working environments. Her recent works have explored the pathways to leadership for Black women.

In my research, I gravitate toward narrative methodologies. In doing so, I am unequivocally aware of whose stories are documented, overlooked, and disseminated over time. Therefore, in my work and practice, I strive to decenter the dominant discourse, expose privilege and other oppressive systems, and deconstruct deficit views of individuals from marginalized communities. In the same vein, this book, *Teaching Women's and Gender Studies*, is filled with

DOI: 10.4324/9781003323327-4

authentic stories that highlight the experiences of women and their fruitful contributions to their communities, physical environments, and their students.

There is a growing focus on controlling which voices are represented in the K-12 curriculum. This timely text highlights the importance of representing diverse voices and experiences and the victories of women through historical and current events. Many of the conversations on feminism occur in higher education. Kathryn Fishman-Weaver and Jill Clingan are making ground-breaking efforts by introducing and making widely accessible culturally relevant feminist perspectives in the K-12 classroom. The scholars highlight important issues on violence against women, communities, and the environment and how acts of violence exist at the intersections of race, gender, and ethnicity. This chapter acknowledges the experiences of not just women in the Global North but also the Global South and documents not only their challenges but offers meaningful ways women have disrupted troubling trends within their social, political, and environmental landscapes.

Centering issues of race, gender, place, and equity, this chapter, "Motherland—History, Health, and Policy Change," charts the changing role of racial, reproductive, gendered, and environmental politics. Furthermore, this chapter reveals that there is a strong need for teachers to gain a deeper understanding of the intersections of race, gender, and its influence on curriculum and classroom interactions. This chapter is an account of how women have been overlooked and disregarded through time and how through such challenges, they have overcome and disrupted racist and sexist acts and advanced. The authors weave together compelling historical accounts that confront racism, gendered norms, and hierarchies that create a hostile environment for women academically, politically, and socially.

In this section, educators learn the feminist, womanist, mujerista and Indigenous ways of understanding our connection to one another and the land. Additionally, educators are encouraged to (1) acknowledge, teach, and share complete histories and counterstories, (2) uphold anti-deficit practices and illuminate gendered and racial dynamics, and (3) enact change within their classrooms and communities. The authors include a list of reflection questions and guided action plans to help educators become more inclusive in their teaching, welcome critical conversations, and initiate change.

Overall, the authors offer new perspectives on how the experiences of women have led to transformational outcomes. Also, this text can serve as an exceptional model for a multifaceted and inclusive perspective on feminism and is an excellent resource for all educators. Most important, this text advocates for educators to understand that "love is a combination of care, commitment, knowledge, responsibility, respect and trust" (hooks, 2002, p. 131) to self, others, and to the motherland.

## Teaching Concept Overview—Motherland: History, Health, and Policy Change

**Unit Purpose:** These next lessons encourage deep thinking about political, environmental, and personal landscapes. In addition to studying gender victories around the world, examining difficult data on maternal health, and considering the gendered effects of our clean water crisis, scholars will also draw connections across these issues. Building on our earlier work around Sustainable Development Goal (SDG) 5, these units also introduce scholars to SDG 3 (health) and SDG 6 (clean water). Finally, scholars engage in a month-long action project in which they apply our focus concepts of advocacy and mothering to make a difference in their local communities.

✔️ **Objectives: By the end of these units, scholars will be able to:**

◆ Analyze case studies on history makers, including Claudette Colvin, Harriet Tubman, Autumn Peltier, and Rukumani (Ruku) Tripathi.

◆ Identify connecting threads across contemporary and global issues, including structural racism, climate change, health disparities, and gender discrimination.

◆ Utilize strengths-based approaches to create research projects on gender victories as well as local and global maternal health issues.

◆ Create and implement an action plan to impact change in their local communities.

**❓ Essential Questions for Scholars**

◆ What does it mean to tell more complete histories?

◆ What do our ancestral history makers teach us about current events?

◆ How can feminist and Indigenous wisdom help us better understand the connection between land and the body?

◆ What is the global landscape for maternal health, and how can I advocate to reduce health disparities?

**⏸ Reflective Questions for Educators**

◆ What lessons and perspectives do I need to incorporate to teach a more complete history?

◆ How can I navigate complex and emotionally charged topics in a safe, brave, and effective way in my classroom?

◆ How do I draw on feminist and Indigenous wisdom in our curricula?

| Activate Prior Knowledge—Claudette Colvin, the Teenager Who Helped Desegregate Montgomery Busses | |
|---|---|
| **Unit 5—Policy Change** | **Unit 6—Maternal Health** |
| Lesson 1—Abolition: History Maker: Harriet Tubman<br>Lesson 2—Global Case Studies: Toward Gender Justice<br>Lesson 3—United States History: Policy Case Studies<br>Lesson 4—History Maker: Autumn Peltier | Lesson 1—Global Maternal Health<br>Lesson 2—History Maker: Rukumani (Ruku) Tripathi, Nepal<br>Lesson 3—Inequities in Maternal Care: United States |
| **Synthesis Project—Impacting Change, Caring for My Community** | |

## Concept Dedications

**Kathryn's Dedication**—I dedicate this chapter to Ms. Tonnesha Pace. I met Ms. Pace my first year teaching. At the time, she was a parent leader in the public K-8 school where I served as a learning and early elementary specialist. Early in the school year, Ms. Pace joined our classroom as a paraprofessional.

The two focus terms for these next two units are *mothering* and *advocacy*. Ms. Pace embodies both concepts with wisdom and purpose. She drew on her experiences and identities as a parent, parent leader, and Black woman in a predominantly Latinx school to mother us all. This work included purposeful advocacy for inclusion, representation, and high expectations for our young scholars with disabilities.

That same year, through the miracle of adoption, I became a mother myself. Ms. Pace helped me step into that role with courage. Later in this chapter, we ask scholars to differentiate between being *fearless* (which is a fiction in my opinion) and *being courageous* (a necessity for everything that matters). Ms. Pace never shied away from difficult topics like racism, ableism, or justice. She approached them head on with a love and grace I continue to try to emulate. As the new mother of a transracial family, I have vivid memories of both my son and I leaning (figuratively and literally) on Ms. Pace's shoulder. Sometimes we cried. Often we laughed. And we always learned something new.

When I think about cultivating a sense of home in my classrooms, I think about these moments and the years that Ms. Pace and I worked together in a sunny classroom in East Oakland, California.

**Jill's Dedication**—I would like to dedicate this chapter to an educator, midwife, and dear friend, Rachel Andresen. When I met Rachel, she was teaching high school English in the town I was living in, and I was teaching composition and literature courses at the local university. I had recently given birth to my first child, Amélie, and Rachel was soon to give birth to her first child, Elanor. We bonded over our love of books and our initiation into new parenthood. A few years later, Rachel became a birth doula, and she was my doula one early morning when my son Jack was born, which was one of the most powerful, beautiful days of my life.

When mothers are in labor, doing one of the most powerful things that a human being can do, they are often at their most vulnerable, as the medical system does not often approach birth from a space of love and trust. As a birth doula, Rachel mothered mothers before, during, and after they delivered their babies, and she also advocated for them so that they had a voice in their maternal care. Now, Rachel is a homebirth midwife, and she continues to live out this calling of love and trust, mothering and advocacy.

In these units, we talk about how being an educator is similar to being a midwife and how our classroom can be a motherland, a safe space of love and trust. Learning, like giving birth, is a space of both power and vulnerability, and I am grateful for Rachel and what her example has taught me about providing a safe space, for both myself and my students, to be both powerful and vulnerable.

## Concept Introduction by Kathryn and Jill

A *motherland* is a place where you or your ancestors were born. It can also be somewhere to which you have a strong emotional attachment. In this chapter, we (Jill and Kathryn) draw on Indigenous wisdom about the land-body connection to explore motherland from a multifaceted perspective. Pulitzer Prize poet Natalie Diaz wrote, "Our lands and our bodies are connected in a way that creates a specific knowing of each. They cannot be parted. They exist as extensions of the other." Diaz is Mojave and an enrolled member of the Gila River Indian community. Drawing on Mojave words, she continues, "The word for earth, land, dirt, is 'amat.' The word for body is 'iimat.' The abbreviations for both are mat-. Mat- is the prefix that begins many Mojave words that describe or are connected to the body and the land" (2014, para 3).

In the following units, scholars meet activists responsible for rewriting history and furthering racial and gender justice across many landscapes: political, environmental, and personal. Social and environmental advocacy work are not mutually exclusive. How we care for the earth and those who call it home are inextricably linked. To close this unit, scholars will engage in a deeper study of the equity and justice work needed around global maternal health.

## Educator Letter for Concept 3—*With Caution and Care*

Dear Valued Educator,

In this connecting space, we (Kathryn and Jill) invite you to think with us about the upcoming chapter content. Brew a cup of tea and pull up a chair, and let's think together about this content and what care might look like **for you** in teaching these complex and difficult topics.

### Your Work Matters
In broad strokes, these next two units are about home. What does home mean? Who and where feels like home? Where do your scholars call home? How can your classroom be a home or *motherland*? These are emotionally and culturally complex questions. You and your scholars may have many different experiences with home. These might be influenced by immigration, travel, housing insecurity, foster care, kinship placements, moving for work, divorce, underemployment, new opportunities, or any number of life changes that shift, complicate, or expand your definition of home.

Our (Kathryn and Jill's) care notes for this chapter center on giving yourself and your scholars space to listen to the different emotions these lessons may stir up.

### Care Strategies for Educators
Unit 3 includes many examples of work to end violence against women. This is heavy and important work. Please see our teaching notes related to addressing violence and sexual violence in the classroom on pp. 22–24.

Unit 4 focuses on maternal health. This is an important global issue. It is also a difficult topic, and your lived experiences may make it deeply personal for you. According to the Mayo Clinic (2021), somewhere between 10% and 20% of pregnancies are reported as ending in miscarriage. However, these statistics may drastically underestimate this number. Many of the readers of this book, educators implementing these lessons, and writers and thought partners who worked on this project have personally experienced or cared for a loved one who has experienced miscarriage or infant loss. If just reading these sentences is difficult for you, please know that you are not alone. We (Kathryn and Jill) want to wrap you in care and offer some cautions before approaching the second unit in this chapter. To this end, below are three strategies to consider now before you even open those lessons.

- **What does self-care mean for you in this unit?** If you know going into this unit that this topic will be personally triggering or difficult to navigate, we encourage you to proceed with care. You may want to meet with a counselor and talk it through. Ask yourself what self-care might mean for you during this unit. If the answer to this is not teaching this unit right now, give yourself permission to say, "That is okay."
- **Set ground rules.** Likewise, the scholars in your classes may also have personal or familial experiences with inadequate maternal health, health disparities, or infant death that you may or may not know about. Proceed with care and compassion for each of them. Set ground rules at the start of these lessons. These might include that everyone has permission to take a break, to care for themselves, to take an activity in a different direction, and even to opt out.
- **Identify supports**. Prior to starting this unit, identify caring professionals in your school who are available to process with *anyone* in need of an extra listening ear. These professionals might include you, a school nurse, counselor, or other mental health professional.

With admiration,

Kathryn and Jill

## Activate Prior Knowledge—Claudette Colvin, the Teenager Who Helped Desegregate Montgomery Busses

 **Thought Questions**
- Create a list of the major social injustices of our time.
- Who and which communities have been harmed by these injustices?
- What would it look like to heal and repair these injustices?
- How long is too long to wait for justice?

Nine months before Rosa Parks' act of resistance led to the Montgomery Bus boycott, 15-year-old Claudette Colvin refused to give up her seat on a segregated bus in Montgomery, Alabama. Black History Month had just ended, and Colvin and her classmates had been studying important Black leaders like Harriet Tubman and Sojourner Truth. Colvin said it was her constitutional right to keep the seat she had paid for (Begnaud & Reardon, 2021). She was handcuffed and arrested, and the case was heard in juvenile court, where a judge declared that Colvin was a "delinquent" and placed her on probation "as a ward of the state pending good behavior."

She continued to work for civil rights and was a plaintiff in the landmark lawsuit that outlawed racial segregation on Montgomery's buses. However, even after the law was overturned, Ms. Colvin never heard that her probation was complete. She waited and kept waiting. Sixty-six years later, in 2021, a judge finally expunged her record.[1]

Ms. Colvin said that although she is now an elderly woman, clearing her name will matter to her children, her grandchildren, and Black children everywhere. She said,

> When I think about why I'm seeking to have my name cleared by the state, it is because I believe if that happened it would show the generation growing up now that progress is possible, and things do get better. It will inspire them to make the world better.
>
> (Associated Press, 2021, para 10)

(▶) **Watch the video "Civil Rights Pioneer Claudette Colvin Has Arrest Records Expunged."** You can find a link in our chapter appendix. Following the video, share your reactions to the following questions.

- ◆ What surprised you in this video?
- ◆ Who are the heroes in this story? Defend your answer. Note: there are multiple answers to this question.
- ◆ What does Ms. Colvin's story teach us about the importance of teaching and celebrating Black History and women's history?
- ◆ What is Claudette Colvin's legacy, and how will you honor that legacy?

| Exit Question: What can our ancestral history makers teach us about current events? In answering this essential question, consider both the personal and political reverberations of those who came before us. | |
| --- | --- |
| **Personally** | **Politically** |
| How have YOUR ancestors influenced your identity and experiences? How do they inspire you to act for justice? | How have those that came before us created more equitable and just policies or practices? What specific contributions of women of color, Black, and Indigenous activists can you name? |

## Unit 5: Policy Change

The term *history* comes from the Greek and Latin *historia,* meaning both to ask and to offer a story or narrative. As Canadian poet Anne Carson reflected, this "asking is not idle. It is when you are asking about something that you realize you yourself have survived it, and so you must carry it" (Gorman, 2021). Presidential inaugural poet Amanda Gorman opened her first full-length poetry collection with a poem called "Ship's Manifest." This poem responds to the questions Carson raised about what history asks of us and the questions historians ask of our world. In Gorman's words: "To be accountable, we must render an account; not what was said, but what was meant. Not the fact, but what was felt" (Gorman, 2021, pp. 1–2).

History is the story of the past, and since the narrative of the past shapes the present and our future, how that story is told—and who tells it—are critical. When whole sections of the population are left out of the story of the past, how does that shape the future? While the origin of the term *history* is not gendered, some feminists use the term *herstory* to draw attention to and center the telling of women's stories. It is essential to tell *herstory* so that the collective narrative you and your peers read, learn, and know contains the depth, breadth, layers, and stories of those who worked toward equity, justice, and freedom.

Yet how present are women's stories, Indigenous stories, young people's stories, the stories of people of color, and the stories of LGBTQIA+ people in our histories? According to historian Dr. Bettany Hughes, women "only occupy around .5% of recorded history," and much of that history is still told from a perspective that perpetuates feminine stereotypes. For example, in reading about Cleopatra, one often encounters a sexualized story that leaves out the truths that Cleopatra was a poet and philosopher who excelled at math (2017). Too often our recorded accounts of history marginalize, erase, or relegate women to supporting roles (Angyal, 2018). Thus, women's stories, accomplishments, and experiences are too often left out of our public histories and scholarly curricula. In fact, in 2017, the Women's History Museum published a report called *Where Are the Women? A Report on the Status of Women in the United States Social Studies Standards,* which analyzed the social studies standards for all 50 states plus Washington, D.C., and found that out of 737 historical figures mentioned, only 178 were women. Trends across the standards include that (1) only the most well-known women of color are studied (and that the telling of their histories is often incomplete and oversimplified); (2) that marginalized groups, including Black, Indigenous, and LGBTQIA+ women, are underrepresented; that women are often portrayed as ancillary rather than central to historical events; and (3) that women's domestic roles are more often studied than their contributions to fields like STEM or politics (2017).

In this unit, you will study both individual biographies and short case studies. Through these readings, you will meet activists, organizers, politicians, and leaders who have written and are actively rewriting history. Many of these leaders were the first from their identity groups to step into specific roles, and all had to step forward with courage and the belief that the world could be different. These leaders come from many different racial, ethnic, cultural, and linguistic backgrounds and many different lived experiences. They teach that change is possible and that none of us works alone. All of these readings invite further reading and research.

## Guiding Questions

- ◆ What can you learn from the visionary activists of today and from those who came before us?
- ◆ How have women changed the course of history through activism and advocacy?
- ◆ How can you be a history maker today?

### Key Term: *Advocacy*

Advocacy is actively supporting a person, cause, or policy. Advocacy means being for something, someone, or a community. In this way, it can be political and public and personal or interpersonal. For example, in our (Kathryn and Jill's) school, we have a motto that "we are for each other." This belief directly translates to the ways we care for and promote each member of our school community. Advocacy and action are directly linked; being an advocate is about what you do to advance an idea or to influence progress or change you believe in.

## Lesson 1: Abolition—History Maker: Harriet Tubman

| Term | Definition |
| --- | --- |
| Abolition | The ending of a practice, system, or institution, often in reference to institutional racism or the systematic denial of human rights such as human enslavement. |
| Underground Railroad | A cooperative system of abolitionists in the United States who worked to support enslaved peoples' escape to the North and Canada before 1863. |

The abolitionist Harriet Tubman was born between 1820 and 1822 in Maryland, a state that still practiced and legally condoned human enslavement. Her parents, along with her and her siblings, were enslaved, and when Tubman was just five years old, she was cruelly sold to a neighboring plantation. A young child herself, Harriet Tubman was forced to labor in childcare and field work, including setting out muskrat traps. As an enslaved person, she experienced and witnessed the evils of slavery firsthand as she lived within its horrors and cruelty. Despite this trauma, Tubman had an indomitable spirit. As a 12-year-old girl, she refused to help an overseer chase an enslaved person who was trying to escape. The overseer threw a two-pound weight at the person running for their freedom, but instead of hitting him, the weight hit Tubman in the head. She was severely injured, and for the rest of her life, she experienced headaches, often collapsed into a deep sleep, and woke up from her sleeping spells remembering vivid dreams that she believed came from God (*Harriet Tubman*, 2018).

Harriet Tubman's legal name was Araminta Ross. She grew up with the nickname "Minty." In September 1849, she changed her name in honor of her mother and to avoid those who would be searching for her when she escaped to Pennsylvania. Although historians do not know precisely how long it took Tubman to make it to freedom, they do know that her dangerous journey was around 90 miles and likely took one to three weeks and that she was assisted by members of the Underground Railroad, a group of advocates who supported the abolitionist cause and who helped enslaved people escape by sheltering them in their homes and escorting them along the Underground Railroad route (*Harriet Tubman*, 2009).

After she stepped across that line into freedom, however, Tubman knew that she wanted to return to help others escape, so she joined the Underground Railroad as a conductor, someone who helped lead enslaved people along the dangerous route to freedom. She disguised herself to remain undetected and, over the course of several years, safely made 13 treacherous and arduous trips back and forth across slavery lines, guiding at least 70 people to free states. She was nicknamed "Moses" after the biblical character who was also known for heroically guiding people out of slavery (*FAQ: Harriet Tubman*, n.d.).

While many people know of her abolitionist work, her service in the Union Army and as a suffragist are lesser known. In 1861, Harriet Tubman became a cook, a nurse, and a spy for the Union army. She was also the first (and only) woman to lead a raid in the Civil War when, in 1863, she, along with a Union general, led Union troops through the Combahee River and into Confederate territory where she helped free over 700 enslaved people (*Role in the Civil War: Harriet Tubman*, n.d.). When the war was over, she moved to New York. There she gave speeches supporting women's right to vote and devoted her life to help take care of older adults, the sick, and others who were marginalized or under-resourced (*Harriet Tubman*, 2009).

## Key Themes—Abolitionism and Courage

Abolition work continues today. While the term *abolition* is often linked to the ending of legal human enslavement in the United States, the work of dismantling systemic racism and promoting intergenerational healing is far from complete. Contemporary abolitionists focus on the ways our justice system, particularly the prison and policing systems, reinforce systemic racism. They call for "a transformative politics, one that centers the agency of Black communities and the struggles caused by the history of legal slavery and its aftermath" (Horton, 2021, para 6). (See especially the work of Ruth Wilson Gilmore and Angela Davis.)

---

 **Thought Question**

◆ How does the abolition movement continue to matter today?

---

Harriet Tubman is a role model for courage. *Courage* comes from the Latin word that means heart. Justice work requires bravery that comes from the heart. Kasi Lemmons, a professor and director of the 2019 biographical film *Harriet,* had this to say about Harriet Tubman and courage:

> I think it's good to be reminded of what can be achieved if your courage outweighs your fear. . . . We bow under the weight of the world and it just seems too much; the problems are insurmountable. But when you look at a story of what one young woman achieved just by

being brave. She wasn't fearless. . . . . She had fear, but she had de-termination, and her courage outweighed her fear, and I think that's what we need in this time right now. Our courage needs to outweigh our fear, and we need to believe that through force of will we can change things. We can change our country.

(Headlee, 2019, 19:30)

---

 **Thought Questions**

◆ What is the difference between being fearless and having courage?
◆ How does courage relate to justice work?

---

### Six-Word Memoir

A memoir is a true story, and a six-word memoir is a very short true story. Popularized by Larry Smith in 2006, the six-word memoir project has become a powerful classroom writing and art prompt that has led to book collections and moving moments of connection and surprise (Daly, 2012). In this activity, we challenge you to write, in just six words, a takeaway from this lesson. You can write this six-word memoir as a sentence, phrases, or a list of words—there are no rules other than that your memoir be connected to one or both of our key themes—courage and abolition—and that it is just six words long. First, do some brainstorming. Consider ideas from the list below or brain-storm some of your own, and then distill those ideas into just six words:

◆ What stood out to you in this lesson?
◆ What are the greatest acts of courage you have seen in your lifetime?
◆ When was the last time you were called on to be brave and felt safe to do so?
◆ Why does ending racism matter to you?
◆ What is your vision for a just world?

Now pare your work down to just six words.

| My Six-Word Memoir |
| --- |
|  |
|  |
|  |
|  |
|  |
|  |

As you continue to refine your memoir, consider adding artwork such as a drawing, painting, or collage. These mixed-media memoirs remind us that your experiences and ideas are so powerful that in just six words, you can inspire others.[2]

## Lesson 2: Global Case Studies—Toward Gender Justice

The term *feminism* is first attributed to French philosopher Charles Fourier in the early 1800s (*Timeline: Women of the World, Unite!*, n.d.). The early usage of the word connects it to women's rights and liberties; that said, it is important to note that feminism often excluded women of color and working-class women. Focusing on women's independent and public identities is historically significant, as this work directly challenged the social belief that women were dependent, subordinate, and ancillary to men and known primarily in their functions as wife, mother, and daughter. The feminist movements in the British colonies and later in the United States focused on legal rights, including suffrage, wages, contracts, and property. In her NPR piece on the etymology of the term *feminism*, Dr. Robin Henry (2015) reports: "Dismantling the legal, political, economic, social and cultural infrastructures of coverture requires not only recognition of women's equality to men, but also acknowledgement of women's individual identities in all matters of life" (para 4). Marie Shear put it a bit more plainly in 1986 when she asserted that "feminism is the radical notion that women are people" (Feminism 101, 2007).  In Unit 1, we (Kathryn and Jill) defined *feminism* as *an affirmation of humanity that seeks freedom from oppression and commits to the full access of social, economic, and political rights and opportunities for all people*.

In this lesson, you will learn about six historical gender victories. This abridged global history points to important context for understanding how feminisms have and continue to influence action. These snapshots of gender victories over the past 100+ years are situated across the globe. As you read them, remember that for every story, there are multitudes of stories in between, some known and many unknown. These victories and steps toward justice are often influenced by the actions of those who came before us. They then continue to have a ripple effect, reverberating for generations after.

### How Can You Contribute to Writing the Ongoing Story of Gender Justice?

**1911—First International Women's Day**

In 1908, 15,000 women marched in New York City to protest against working hours and unequal pay and to demand the right to vote. A few years later, Clara Zetkin proposed the establishment of an International Women's Day, which, she argued, "must be *international* . . . because oppression cuts across national borders. It is *women's* day because . . . the inhuman burden of global capitalism weighs with special heaviness on women" (Nassar & Gjesdal, 2022). On March 8, 1911, the first International Women's Day was celebrated in Austria, Denmark, Germany, and Switzerland to support the fight for voting and labor rights, and over one million men and women attended rallies to bring attention to and advocate for gender equality. In 1975, the United Nations (UN) declared March 8 as International Women's Day (*History of International Women's Day*, n.d.).

**Key Figure:** Clara Zetkin

## 1929—The "Women's War" in Nigeria

Prior to British colonization in eastern Nigeria, both men and women held powerful roles in the area's political landscape. The British destabilized women's power, however, when they appointed local men as warrant chiefs to impose British law on the Igboo people. When the British ordered a census to be taken that would have led to unfair market taxes on women, an older woman named Nwanyeruwa refused to give information about her household to the census taker. She then informed the women's assembly that the British planned to tax women, and the Igboo women organized a protest by passing palm leaves to each other with a secret message about the protest. When the appointed day for the protest arrived, 10,000 women descended upon the warrant chief of Oloko and demanded that they not be taxed. As a result, the warrant chief was removed from power, and the market taxes were removed (Marinaro, 2021). This success sparked protests in other parts of Nigeria, and became known as the "Women's War" because the movement demanded change for the ways women were being treated unfairly. Although the Women's War was peaceful, the British police officers and troops fired into the protest, killing 50 women and wounding 50 more. Despite this horrific ending to these protests, the momentum of the Women's War helped remove many warrant chiefs from office and eventually led to the Igboo people regaining some power from the British (*Igbo Women Campaign for Rights [The Women's War] in Nigeria, 1929*, n.d.).

**Key Figure:** Nwanyeruwa

## 1960—Las Mariposas in the Dominican Republic

Minerva, María Teresa, and Patria Mirabel—three sisters known as Las Mariposas (the butterflies)—were part of a protest movement against Rafael Trujillo's corrupt and violent dictatorship in the Dominican Republic. The sisters were murdered on November 25, 1960, and after their murder, they became martyrs for the resistance cause. Their activism and subsequent assassination ordered by Trujillo continues to inspire gender advocates around the world. In 1999, the UN declared November 25 the International Day for the Elimination of Violence Against Women (Pruitt, 2021). The campaign has continued to gain global traction and grown in scope to now include 16 days of intentional global activism against gender violence annually.

**Key Figures:** Minerva, María Teresa, and Patria Mirabel

**1979—The Convention on the Elimination of All Forms of Discrimination Against Women (CEDAW; Nicknamed the "Women's Bill of Rights") Adopted by the United Nations**

The Convention on the Elimination of All Forms of Discrimination Against Women (CEDAW) "defines and constitutes discrimination against women and sets up an agenda for national action to end such discrimination" (*Convention on the Elimination of All Forms of Discrimination against Women*, n.d.).
  According to *UN Women*,

> The Convention provides the basis for realizing equality between women and men through ensuring women's equal access to, and equal opportunities in, political and public life—including the right to vote and to stand for election—as well as education, health and employment. . . . The Convention is the only human rights treaty which affirms the reproductive rights of women and targets culture and tradition as influential forces shaping gender roles and family relations. It affirms women's rights to acquire, change or retain their nationality and the nationality of their children . . . [and requires that countries who ratify this Constitution will] take appropriate measures against all forms of traffic in women and exploitation of women. (*Convention on the Elimination of All Forms of Discrimination against Women*, n.d.)

**Key Figure:** United Nations Commission on the Status of Women

**1992—Rigoberta Menchú: First Indigenous Woman to Receive the Nobel Peace Prize**

In 1992, Rigoberta Menchú was the first Indigenous woman awarded the Nobel Peace Prize for "recognition of her work for social justice and ethno-cultural reconciliation based on respect for the rights of Indigenous peoples" (*Meet Nobel Peace Laureate Rigoberta Menchú Tum*, 2017). Menchú grew up in a Native family in Guatemala that fought for the rights of Indigenous people. Her father, mother, and brother were all killed for protesting the violent and corrupt acts of the Guatemalan dictatorial government. After her family was killed, Menchú fled to Mexico, and when she was 23 years old, she published *I, Rigoberta Menchú: An Indian Woman in Guatemala*, which highlighted the plight of the Mayan people in Guatemala and catapulted the atrocities of the civil war in Guatemala to international attention (*Meet Nobel Peace Laureate Rigoberta Menchú Tum*, 2017).

**Key Figure:** Rigoberta Menchú

## 2006, 2017—#MeToo Movement

The #MeToo movement is a powerful example of the global impact of a peaceful and nonviolent protest. "Me too" began in 2006 when nonprofit executive and women's advocate Tarana Burke coined this phrase to raise awareness about sexual harassment and assault and to provide women a space in which to tell their stories and find solidarity in realizing that they are not alone (Burke, 2020). In 2017, actress Alyssa Milano tweeted the phrase as a hashtag after Harvey Weinstein was accused of multiple counts of sexual harassment, and this started a global movement. #MeToo then took on a life of its own, as people from all over the world used this hashtag to expand Burke's initial purpose of raising awareness around sexual assault. It has now been used by more than 19 million people. Writers in the #MeToo movement share their stories with the hope of letting victims know that they are not alone. This hashtag has now been translated into many languages, encouraging people all over the world to share their stories and put an end to violence against women. In 2017, *Time Magazine* named Tarana Burke and the "silence breakers" their person of the year.

**Key Figures:** Tarana Burke and Alyssa Milano

# Global Case Studies: Infographic Project—Toward Gender Justice

**Name** _____ **Date**_____

**Directions:** Create an educational infographic about one of the global case studies from this lesson. This project requires you to *go beyond* the information included in our curriculum. Working alone or in small groups, learn as much as possible about the context, leaders, and impact surrounding your chosen event. Your final infographic should fit neatly on one page. You might use a free design software such as Canva.

| All infographics should include the following: |
| --- |
| Name of the event |
| A thesis statement on why this event is significant |
| Location of the event and locations impacted by the event |
| ◆ Be able to identify these locations on a map. |
| Date(s) of the event |
| A list of the key figure(s) associated with the event |
| A brief summary of the event |
| A reflective statement connecting this event to contemporary work toward gender justice |
| References |

This curriculum includes several case studies for you to select from; however, this is a woefully incomplete list! If you have another relevant event (particularly that originated outside your home country) that you would like to research, let your teacher know.

## Lesson 3: United States History—Policy Case Studies

Former Supreme Court Justice Ruth Bader Ginsburg (1933–2020) said, "Women's rights are an essential part of the overall human rights agenda, trained on the equal dignity and ability to live in freedom all people should enjoy" (American Civil Liberties Union, n.d.). Justice Ginsburg was a champion for women's rights and human rights during her work with courts. She also served as the co-founder of the Women's Rights Project at the American Civil Liberties Union (ACLU). In this lesson, you will explore some of the policy changes and historic events in the United States that have led to increased access and representation and expanded rights for women and other marginalized communities.

### 1920—Ratification of the 19th Amendment

**Primary Source Text:** *The 19th Amendment*

*The right of citizens of the United States to vote shall not be denied or abridged by the United States or by any state on account of sex. Congress shall have power to enforce this article by appropriate legislation (U.S. Const. amend. XVIV).*

True or false? The 19th Amendment guaranteed all women the right to vote. This is false. In our continued effort to teach a more complete history, this policy case study points to the women the suffrage movement left out and celebrates Black, Indigenous, and Latina women who fought for more inclusive voting rights. The fight for women's suffrage began in the mid-19th century. For decades, women picketed, protested, wrote, marched, and engaged in civil disobedience as they fought for a law that granted women the right to vote. Finally, after Congress passed the 19th Amendment in 1919, enough states approved the amendment that it was ratified in 1920. Even though the ratification of the 19th Amendment was a key victory for the women's suffrage movement, barriers still remained. Twenty-six million women were granted the right to vote in the 1920 presidential election, but only 36% of them did so, partly because they had to pass literacy tests, pay poll taxes, meet lengthy residency requirements, and overcome the intimidation of the voting process. Women of color faced even more obstacles. Seventy-five percent of African American women were still not allowed to vote due to state constitutions that forbade them of this right, and it was not until 1965, when President Lyndon B. Johnson signed the Voting Rights Act into law, that discriminatory voting prerequisites were outlawed. In addition, Native American women were not even granted citizenship until 1924, and first-generation

Asian-American women were not granted citizenship until 1952 (*Nineteenth Amendment to the United States Constitution*, n.d.). Despite these egregious injustices against women, the ratification of the 19th Amendment was an important step toward gender equality. However, the fight and debate for voting rights continues today. The Supreme Court ruling on the 2013 Voting Rights Act allows states to enact voter ID laws. These restrictions have been cited as specifically targeting marginalized communities, particularly communities of color (Levine & Rao, 2020).

**Key Figures:** Elizabeth Cady Stanton, Lucretia Mott, Susan B. Anthony, Sojourner Truth, and Ida B. Wells-Barnett

**1923—Equal Rights Amendment Introduced to United States Congress**

**Primary Source Text:** *The Equal Rights Amendment*

*Equality of rights under the law shall not be denied or abridged by the United States or by any State on account of sex. The Congress shall have the power to enforce, by appropriate legislation, the provisions of this article* (National Organization for Women, n.d.).

The purpose of the Equal Rights Amendment (ERA) is to provide equal legal status regardless of gender and prevent discrimination based on sex. This amendment was first introduced to Congress in 1923 by the National Women's political party, but it was not approved by the U.S. Senate until March 1972. The Equal Rights Amendment, which states, "Equality of rights under the law shall not be denied or abridged by the United States or by any state on account of sex," passed in Congress but still needs the vote of one more state to become the 27th Amendment to the Constitution. In 2020, the ERA Amendment was finally ratified by the required 38 states, but because not enough states had ratified the amendment by the 1982 deadline, this amendment is still not a part of the United States Constitution.

There is still hope, however, that this important amendment will be passed into U.S. law. In January of 2021, a bipartisan, joint resolution was introduced to Congress that would get rid of the 1982 expiration date and allow this amendment to finally be ratified[3] (Thulin, 2020).

**Key Figures:** Alice Paul, Crystal Eastman, Bella Abzug, Gloria Steinem, Kate Millett, Shirley Chisholm, and Martha Griffiths

## 1955—Rosa Parks, Mother of the Civil Rights Movement

In 1955 in Montgomery, Alabama, Rosa Parks refused to give up her seat on a bus to a White male passenger who was boarding. She was then arrested and lost in court when she challenged this act of segregation. Others had also practiced similar acts of resistance on segregated busses, including Claudette Colvin (see pp. 111–12). These arrests fueled the subsequent year-long Montgomery bus boycott, which is often cited as the beginning of the civil rights movement in the United States (*Rosa Parks*, 2018).

Called "the mother of the civil rights movement," Rosa Parks stated on her 77th birthday that "I would like to be known as a person who is concerned about freedom and equality and justice and prosperity for all people" (The National Women's Hall of Fame, n.d.).

This book contains numerous examples of the ways Black feminists have demanded advocacy work that inextricably links racial justice and gender justice. Rosa Parks is an important thought leader in this movement.

**Key Figures:** Rosa Parks and Claudette Colvin

## 1994—Violence Against Women Act: Multiple Reauthorizations

In 1994, United States President Bill Clinton signed into law the Violence Against Women Act (VAWA). This act emerged from the grassroots effort of domestic abuse and sexual assault advocates who petitioned Congress to create and pass this law (*Violence Against Women Act*, n.d.). This act provides federal funds and protection for women from domestic abuse, sexual assault, stalking, and rape. This act also provides resources necessary to educate communities about violence against women and administer justice to those who commit acts of violence against women. According to an article in *Journal of Women's Health*,

> One of the greatest successes of VAWA is its emphasis on a coordinated community response to domestic violence, sex dating violence, sexual assault, and stalking; courts, law enforcement, prosecutors, victim services, and the private bar currently work together in a coordinated effort that did not exist before at the state and local levels.
>
> (Modi et al., 2014, p. 253)

This act was reauthorized in 2000, 2005, and 2013. In 2021, it was expanded to limit access to guns for those who have been convicted of stalking.

During the writing of this book, it came under reauthorization again. If passed, this latest reauthorization will reauthorize VAWA through 2026. The new draft "includes provisions to strengthen rape prevention and education efforts, provide legal funding and increase support for marginalized communities like LGBTQ survivors and 'expand special criminal jurisdiction by tribal courts to cover non-Native perpetrators of sexual assault'" (Wise, 2022, para 9).

**Key Figures:** Eleanor Smeal and Esta Soler

## January 2017—Women's March on Washington

Following the 2016 election, Teresa Shook, a grandmother and retired lawyer living in Hawaii, created a Facebook event for a women's march in Washington, D.C. She invited 40 of her friends, and by the next morning, over 10,000 people had RSVPed that they would be attending. Several organizers from many different expert areas, professional backgrounds, and personal identities heard of Shook's events and started organizing (Stein, 2017).

On January 17, 2017, approximately 5 million people joined together in various cities across the United States and in 30 countries around the world for the Women's March to support and protect the long-held feminist value that "women's rights are human rights." The Women's March advocates for the human rights of all people regardless of gender, sexual orientation, race, immigration status, or religion. The Women's March of 2017 was the largest recorded protest in United States history (*Women's March*, 2018), and in the United States, as well as all around the world, it represented a unifying call to action and activism.

You can read more about the organizers listed, as well as others who contributed to the success of this event and sister events across the country and globe, at the link included in our chapter appendix.

**Key Figures:** Carmen Perez, Tamika Mallory, Linda Sarsour, Bob Bland, and Teresa Shook

# Living Timeline—Gender Victories in the United States

Name _____ Date_____

## What is a living timeline?

This activity culminates in an interactive learning event. Each presenter or research team will prepare a research station to educate visitors about the policy or event they studied. As opposed to creating a poster that stands for itself, scholars should be active presenters at the event—visitors are encouraged to ask questions. Set up your classroom (or event space) so that the earliest gender victory is the first that visitors encounter and the latest gender victory the last.

While this living timeline is specific to gender victories in the United States, this same format can be used for a variety of historical events. Events such as these help expand our teaching of more complete histories beyond our classroom community. As a class, decide on who you want to invite to this living timeline. Ideas include families, same-grade classes, and younger students.

**Directions:** Select one of the historic events from this lesson to study at greater depth. Learn as much as possible about the event or policy and prepare a research station on the event. Your station might include a poster or other materials; however, the most important resource at your station is you (and your research team), as you will serve as the historical expert(s). Visitors will view posters and other materials you have created and ask you questions about your event or policy. If you have another relevant event you would like to research and include in our Living Timeline, just let your teacher know!

| Research stations should include the following: |
| --- |
| Name of the event or policy |
| A thesis statement describing (1) why this policy or event was significant and (2) why continued justice work is needed<br><br>◆ What did the policy or event accomplish?<br>◆ What didn't the policy or event accomplish and/or who did this policy leave out? |
| The conditions (e.g. people and forces) that made this policy or event possible |

Date(s) of the event

A summary of the event or policy

Brief biographies of the key figure(s) associated with the event

A reflective statement connecting this event to contemporary work toward gender justice

References (especially primary source accounts) used in preparing your research station

## Lesson 4: History Maker: Autumn Peltier

 **Thought Questions**

◆ Is water a fundamental human right?
◆ What is your relationship to water?
◆ How often do you think about access to clean water?

### United Nations' Sustainable Development Goal 6

According to the World Health Organization, one in three people in the world do not have safe drinking water available to them. Even more do not have access to safe sanitation services and handwashing facilities (*1 in 3 People Globally Do Not Have Access to Safe Drinking Water—UNICEF, WHO*, 2019). Depending on your lived experiences, culture, and context, your answers to these opening thought questions may vary widely.

If I (Kathryn) had answered these three thought questions when I was in high school, I would have said that water was a fundamental human right; however, I only understood access to it abstractly. Growing up, we never had our water turned off nor did I have to worry about the safety of water from our tap. If asked, I might have talked about my first experience sanitizing water to make it safe for drinking, which happened on a junior high scouting trip. Mostly, though, I took clean water for granted, taking long baths, filling soup pots with more water than was necessary, playing in the hose in our front yard, and swimming joyously in a community pool all summer long.

I was an adult the first time I traveled to a place where access to clean water was limited. This context opened my eyes to how tenuous access to clean water is and helped me understand the importance of infrastructure in ways I hadn't considered before. If I were to answer these questions now, my answers would be very different. The experiences I have had traveling to different communities, working and learning with students from around the world, and paying more attention to our vulnerable ecosystems have taught me (1) what a privilege it is to have access to clean and safe water and (2) how limited and fragile this access is. In recent years, my hometown has also experienced several boiling orders and recommendations to reduce water usage. Much like the air I breathe, the water of my childhood has changed, too.

Kathryn's experience is not unique. In recent years, news stories within the United States have exposed just how limited and fragile access to clean water can be. In 2014, the people of Flint, Michigan, including thousands of pregnant women and around 30,000 children, were exposed to water that was polluted with toxic levels of lead (Green, 2019). In January 2022 in Jackson,

Mississippi, a community that is often under a boil order, thousands of students could not go to school. Their schools closed due to little to no water pressure which meant that they could not cook meals, flush toilets, or wash their hands. The year before, thousands of people in this community had been without water for weeks because a storm had shut down the city's water treatment plant (James, 2022). The water crises in both Flint and Jackson demonstrate how oppression is layered across race, gender, socio-economic status, and age. Communities of color, women, children, and low-income families were all disproportionately and dangerously affected by these crises.

Heraclitus, the ancient Greek philosopher, said, "You never step into the same river twice—both the river and our lived experiences are constantly changing." All the different experiences you or your classmates have with your relationship to water and infrastructure are valid and important starting places for this lesson.

---

**United Nations' Sustainable Development Goal 6—Summary**

The target of the UNs' SDG 6 is to "ensure availability and sustainable management of water and sanitation for all."

While access to clean water is a fundamental human right, it is an especially important issue to women and girls, as they suffer the most without access to clean water. According to the UN,

> In 80 percent of households with water shortages, women and girls are responsible for water collection. This often means traveling long distances and carrying heavy loads, in some cases with high risk of violence. The time required can pull girls out of school and leave women with fewer options to earn an income.

> Women are also the ones who end up caring for individuals who become sick because of unclean water, and when women give birth, the lack of clean water can result in sickness and death for both mothers and their babies
> Access to clean water is a fundamental human right.

Source *SDG 6: Ensure Availability and Sustainable Management of Water and Sanitation for All, n.d.*

---

### History Maker—Autumn Peltier

 **Thought Questions**

- ◆ Why is water important?
- ◆ Do you have any special memories that include water?
- ◆ How would you respond to the statement "Water is sacred"?

---

Indigenous wisdom draws on a deep physical and spiritual connection with the land and with our ancestors. "Many indigenous groups refer to their unique relationship with their particular territory as 'I belong to this land,' as opposed to the classic Western articulation, 'this land belongs to me'" (Bishop, 2001). As stewards of land rather than conquerors of it, Indigenous wisdom reminds people that earth and water are sacred and that the connection to them is sacred, as well. The violence of colonization (see p. 39) has unjustly removed many Indigenous people from their homes while also destroying and polluting the lands. Young Indigenous activists are rising up to protect the land of their ancestors for themselves and future generations.

Autumn Peltier (2004–) is an Anishinaabe Indigenous water rights activist. She lives in Canada on Lake Huron and is a member of Wikwemikong First Nation in Ontario. She is the Chief Water Commissioner for Anishinabek Nation, has received several awards connected to her advocacy work, and has been nominated three times for the International Children's Peace Prize (Gallant, 2020). Growing up around one of the largest freshwater lakes in the world, Peltier realized the importance of clean water as both a life-giving and sacred source. She began attending ceremonies with her mother and aunt when she was a young girl, and at one water ceremony, when she was eight years old, she went into a restroom that had signs all over the walls warning that there was a boil order and not to drink the water or even use it to wash hands. She was shocked and sad to learn that on this sacred space, in this sacred land, and at a water ceremony, no less, the water had not been safe to drink or use for over 20 years. Peltier was distraught to think about people who had been under a boil order for years, for people who had to walk miles to get clean water, and for children who were growing up without safe water to drink, so she began her mission as an advocate for clean water (CBC Kids News, 2020, 0:58).

Four years later, in 2017, when Peltier was presenting a gift to Justin Trudeau, the Prime Minister of Canada, she began to cry and told him that she was disappointed in how he was not protecting water for Indigenous people and that he had broken his promises to them. He told her that he would try to do better (CBC Kids News, 2020, 2:17). A year later, in 2018, when Peltier was 13 years old, she gave a speech about clean water in New York to leaders of the UN who were beginning the UN Decade of Water campaign (CBC News, 2018). Watch Peltier's address to the UN (the link to this video is in the appendix) and then discuss the following questions in a small group of your peers:

**Post-Watching Discussion Questions**

◆ How does Peltier's work connect to SDG 6?

◆ Why does Peltier believe that water is sacred?

◆ *Odena* is the Anishinaabe word that means "where your heart is." Peltier said that her heart is in her community, her land, and her water. What do you think this means? What would this philosophy look like in action?

◆ In the video, Peltier stated that one day she will be an ancestor, and she wants future generations to know that she used her voice to fight for clean water. Someday you will be an ancestor, too. How do you want future generations to know how you used your voice?

## Connecting Deeper Through Poetry

If someone were to ask you if you love the earth, what would you say? What about if someone asked you if you thought the earth loved you back? When Robin Wall Kimmerer, a scientist, professor, writer, and member of the Citizen Potawatomi Nation, asked her students this question, she found that her students had a hard time answering it. However, when she asked the question, "What do you suppose would happen *if* people believed this crazy notion that the earth loved them back?" her students had many responses (2013, p. 124).

 **Thought Questions**

◆ Do you believe the earth loves you back?

◆ What would happen if people believed that the earth, both its land and its water, loved them back?

Peltier said that "water is the lifeblood of mother earth" (Global News, 2018, 1:47). Water is our lifeblood, too. As water twists, turns, and flows through creeks, rivers, lakes, and oceans to feed the earth, the earth then uses that water to sustain us, as well. Indigenous wisdom teaches us that when we destroy the water and the earth, we are destroying ourselves. Likewise, when we care for the water and for the earth, we are caring for ourselves (Garrison Institute, 2016). People and lands are intricately and intimately connected. When Peltier participates in a water ceremony, she prays for the water, hoping that one day it is clean (CBC Kids News, 2020, 0:10). Regardless of your own spirituality, can you expand your hope to something bigger than you, something as big as the ocean or the planet we call home? Some call this kind of hope a prayer; others call it a meditation or intention. This can look like paying attention, noticing, and appreciating. This can sound like a song or even a poem.

Deborah Miranda is a Native American poet, writer, and professor who, like Peltier, seeks to protect the earth's vulnerable spaces. In her poem "Prayer of Prayers: For the Water Protectors at Standing Rock,"[4] Miranda suggests that poetry is a rallying call to action and that "the planet is a prayer" (line 32).

Reflect on what you have learned about land and water. Write a meditation, intention, prayer, or a poem on access to clean water, progress toward SDG 6, our connection to the land and water, or an answer to the question Kimmerer asked her students: "What would happen if people believed that the earth loved them back?"

## Unit 6: Maternal Health

The health and wellbeing of families during pregnancy, childbirth, and the postnatal period is essential to thriving communities (World Health Organization, n.d.-b). According to the UN, maternal health is a "fundamental human right" and is also "essential to reducing poverty (SDG 1), ensuring healthy lives (SDG 3), achieving gender equality (SDG 5), and underpins many other global goals" (Green, 2018). Maternal health is not just a women's issue[5]; rather, —improving maternal health has a direct impact on individuals, families, health care systems, and nations.

Unfortunately, maternal health is not always a priority. As scholars will learn in the following lessons, almost 300,000 women die of maternal health complications every year, and the majority of these deaths are preventable (*Maternal Mortality*, 2019). Most of these deaths occur in low-income countries (LICs), but even in middle- and upper-middle income countries such as the United States, maternal deaths are rising, particularly due to systemic racism in marginalized communities (*Working Together to Reduce Black Maternal Mortality*, n.d.). The maternal health statistics included in the following lessons are heart-wrenching and unacceptable. And yet, within this context, there are bright spots of hope, as health professionals and advocates are fighting to improve maternal health outcomes.

I (Jill) used to be immersed in the maternal health world as a doula, which means that I helped women as they went through labor and provided them with emotional and physical support. I sat in front of them, held their hands, looked into their eyes, and breathed with them through contractions. I spent hours squeezing their hips to relieve the pain of back labor. When they told me that they didn't think they could keep going, I walked the hospital halls with them and assured them that yes, they *could* keep going. And they did. I wasn't a midwife, but the word "midwife" means "with woman." As I supported women in labor, I was just "with" them. I couldn't make their babies come any faster. I couldn't take away their pain. But I was with them through that pain. And then, when their babies were born and the pain was forgotten, I was "with them" in their joy.

In a lot of ways, educators are like midwives (Belenky et al., 1997). Just as I (Jill) could not take away the pain of the laboring women that I cared for, we cannot take away the pain our scholars experience, either. But, just as I was with women as they struggled through labor, so, too, can educators find ways to be "with" scholars when they are struggling. They can offer a safe space before and after school and during passing periods and lunch. They can lend an empathic ear and connect scholars and families to wraparound services. They can give support and encouragement as young people explore new and challenging ideas and give birth to their own ideas (Belenky et al., 1997). Together, educators can be "with" scholars in both their struggles and their joys.

At the beginning of this unit, we (Jill and Kathryn) defined "motherland" as not only a place where one is born but also a place where one feels a strong emotional attachment, and for some students, this "motherland" may be your classroom. While birth is an important part of everyone's story, biology is not the only way that families are made. Families can take many diverse shapes—some are made through adoption, kinship care, foster care, and community approaches. As you introduce this unit to your class, assure scholars that this classroom is a brave and affirming space, a "motherland," where all lived experiences are valid and where we can explore ideas and concepts together.

**Key Term: *Mothering***

*Mothering* is a verb that means to care, provide, nurture, and protect. While the term is often used to refer to mothers with their children, mothering is not only for those who birth babies or are called "mothers." The term "mothering" can also apply to an individual of any gender who cares, provides for, nurtures, and protects another. Many types of relationships can involve mothering, including the care, nurturing, and protection of a teacher, physical or mental health care worker, spiritual leader, mentor, or peer. Mothering can also extend outside of physical relationships. For example, just as Mother Earth mothers our communities, you can engage in a reciprocal relationship with the earth where you care for (mother) the land, water, and other resources.

**Lesson 1: Global Maternal Health**

 **Thought Questions**

◆ How would you define *maternal health*?

◆ Why do you think maternal health is important for individuals, families, and society?

◆ What are some potentially harmful effects of a lack of quality maternal health care?

| Term | Definition |
|---|---|
| Maternal health | The physical, emotional, and medical health of child-bearing people during pregnancy, childbirth, and the postnatal period. |
| Maternal mortality ratio (MMR) | According to the World Health Organization, the number of maternal deaths during a given time period per 100,000 live births. . . . It depicts the risk of maternal death relative to the number of live births and essentially captures the risk of death in a single pregnancy or a single live birth. (World Health Organization, n.d.-a) |
| Low-income countries (LICs) | The World Health Organization and the World Bank have moved away from referring to countries as "developing" or "developed" and now categorize countries by their gross domestic product (GDP) and gross national income. Using these statistics, countries can be classified as low income, middle income, or upper-middle income. Many of the LICs discussed in these lessons are located in the Global South. The income statistics are also imperfect, as some emerging economies have trouble estimating their GDP and as some more advanced economies have stark inequities within their countries. As with all the categorization, specificity matters. If you are researching a specific country, name that country. |

The UNs' SDG 3 is to "ensure healthy lives and promote well-being for all at all ages" (United Nations, n.d.-a). One component of SDG 3 is to improve the maternal health of women. The target for this SDG is to decrease the global MMR (which is the maternal death rate per 100,000 live births) to fewer than 70 per 100,000 live births (World Health Organization, n.d.).

**Statistics on Global Maternal Health from the United Nations**

◆ Over 40% of all countries have fewer than 10 medical doctors per 10,000 people; over 55% of countries have fewer than 40 nursing and midwifery personnel per 10,000 people.

◆ Every day in 2017, approximately 810 women died from preventable causes related to pregnancy and childbirth.

◆ Ninety-four percent of all maternal deaths occur in low and lower-middle income countries.

◆ Young adolescents (ages 10–14) face a higher risk of complications and death as a result of pregnancy than other women.

◆ The MMR—the proportion of mothers that do not survive childbirth compared with those who do—in lower income regions is still 14 times higher than in the higher income regions.

◆ In Northern Africa, Eastern Asia, and Southern Asia, the MMR has declined by about two-thirds.

Source: www.un.org/sustainabledevelopment/health/

◆ These are heavy statistics. Let's take an emotional temperature check. What do you need to help process this information? How are you feeling?

◆ What surprises you about these statistics?

◆ Throughout these lessons, we focus on radical hope. Look at this list again. Where are the opportunities for hope? What actions need to follow to bring these possibilities to fruition?

## Maternal Health Care in Low-Income Nations

The MMR for women in LICs is significantly higher than the MMR in middle- and high-income nations. According to the United Nations Population Fund (UNPFA), one woman dies every two minutes from a pregnancy or childbirth-related cause, and "for every woman who dies, an estimated 20 or 30 encounter injuries, infections or disabilities. Most of these deaths and injuries are entirely preventable" (*Maternal Health*, n.d.). Progress is being made. Between 2000 and 2017, the MMR lowered by 38% (*Maternal Mortality*, 2019). Much work is left to be done, however, to reach the SDG target. Because of the MMR disparity, a great deal of this work focuses on increasing access to quality health care for women, especially in the Global South. The geographical areas with the highest MMR are sub-Saharan Africa, South Asia, and Latin America and the Caribbean.

## MMR Research Project—Radical Hope

The following class project asks you to learn more about a country with a high MMR. Before beginning this work, let's pause to consider how research has affected LICs in general and communities of color in particular. Often in high school, most of your exposure to research, particularly conducting research, happens in your science classes, using the scientific method. In this kind of research:

- ◆ Who is seen as the knower?
- ◆ Who tells the story?
- ◆ Who has the most power?
- ◆ What is valued?

The scientific method has an important place in knowledge production, but it isn't the only way to approach research. It is also not always as objective as it might seem. The ways we approach research matters. WGST researchers seek to engage in this work without causing more damage to marginalized communities. This requires a reframing of these questions to honor and center community knowledge and strengths in research. Activist Eve Tuck (2009) suggests that failing to engage in this critical and humanizing thinking about research contributes to "damage-centered frameworks." This happens when a researcher studies a challenge and reports that people, communities, or whole countries are broken. The "conclusions" that follow this kind of study often suggest that the community is in need of saving or rescuing typically by White and affluent groups, organizations, and ways of knowing. Damage-centered frameworks:

- ◆ perpetuate hierarchies and "single stories" (Adichie, 2009);
- ◆ seldom create sustainable change;
- ◆ disempower the groups they have set out to "help";
- ◆ and contribute to an ongoing and *damaging* narrative about race, ethnicity, and poverty (Tuck, 2009).

As scholars, we can—and must—do better. When you engage in research, do so from a place of radical hope, contributing to what Tuck (2009) calls "desire-based frameworks." In my (Kathryn's) research, I describe this as the difference between doing research *on* a community and doing research *with* a community. Instead of positioning the researcher as the knower, I advocate for frameworks where the communities we study and the community leaders (including youth leaders) are respected as knowers. In such a framework, I often engage in co-research where the facilitator serves as a humble learner (Fishman-Weaver, 2018).

This following project invites you to think about what desire-based research might look like in a geographical area with a high MMR. Begin this project by learning more about one of the countries listed below. Specificity matters in research. As your project continues, focus your learning on a specific community or group within these larger geographical areas and fill out the upcoming chart.

- What can you learn about the status of maternal health in this community?
- What strengths can you identify?
- What data is missing?
- If you were to engage in a research project on maternal health in this community, how would you do so from a place of radical hope?
- What strengths do you notice in your research?
- If given the chance, who are the community members you would you want to learn from?
- What conditions might contribute to sustaining change?

After you have filled out your chart, be prepared to present your findings to the rest of your class.

Begin by learning more about one of these countries with a high MMR and then zero on a specific community of interest:

- Sub-Saharan Africa—South Sudan, Chad, Sierra Leone, Nigeria, Central African Republic, Somalia
- South Asia—Afghanistan, Bangladesh, Bhutan, India, Pakistan
- Latin America and the Caribbean—Haiti, Guyana, Bolivia, Guatemala, Suriname

Note: Helpful internet sites to begin this project include the United Nations and World Health Organization websites.

Name _____    Date _____

| MMR Research Project—Radical Hope | |
|---|---|
| **Geographical Area:**<br>**Country:**<br>**Community:** | |
| **Culture**<br>What have you learned about this country? Consider culture, language, traditions, religion, geography, arts, values, etc. | |
| **Communities**<br>What specific communities or groups would you like to learn more about? | |
| **Maternal Health Data**<br>What statistics or data can you find about maternal health related to the country or community you are studying? What data are missing? What questions does this data raise for you? | |
| **Challenges or Barriers**<br>What are some of the challenges or barriers to maternal health that you see reported in the sites you are reading? If you were to continue in this research, how would you learn more about these challenges or barriers? | |

**Community Strengths**
What strengths have you identified related to maternal health? Is there a change maker in this community's history who helped pave the way for conversations and changes concerning maternal health? Who are the community leaders engaged in health care and education work? What would you want to learn from these leaders?

**Radical Hope**
If you were able to continue this research project in-country with the community you are studying, what would you want to learn? Who would you want to meet? What places would you want to see? How would you approach the project as a humble learner?

**Resources**
Where did you find your information for this project?

## Lesson 2: History Maker: Rukumani (Ruku) Tripathi, Nepal

**Teaching Note**

**Proceed with care**—In addition to discussing maternal death, the next two lessons also discuss health challenges related to the COVID pandemic. These sensitive subjects may be personally triggering for you and/or scholars in your class. So many families suffered great losses during the COVID pandemic. This may be a lesson where you employ some or all of the care ground rules established at the start of this unit, such as working directly with a school counselor, giving lots of processing space for the content, chunking these lessons, or skipping sections altogether.

**Proceed with hope**—Since the dawn of time, families have grown through birth. Each of the scholars in your classes arrived on this planet through birth. The following lessons share difficult and heavy statistics about health care systems in need of repair and reimagining. They share about preventable deaths. Processing statistics, particularly emotionally laden statistics like those in the following lessons, can be challenging. It is easy to move to false universals. We (Kathryn and Jill) want to help you address this head on and to encourage your classes to take a collective breath. We are particularly thinking of the Black, Indigenous, and LGBTQIA+ scholars and families in your school communities. While health disparities are present and concerning, not all Black, Indigenous, and LGBTQIA+ families experience trauma or loss during their birthing process. Consistent with this book's commitment to radical hope, we believe it is important to tell stories of joy, celebration, and possibility. The following lessons give you a starting place for learning about community health workers, advocates, and others who are engaged in transformative care work. Don't stop there. We also encourage you to bring health care workers, parents, and advocates into your classrooms to share their great works and to affirm young people who want to make the world a healthier place for families.

### Interactive Reading—Midwives in Nepal

"As one of the first midwives in Nepal," said Rukumani (Ruku) Tripathi,

I am always concerned with the equality and welfare of women. Being born in a country where gender inequality is present in every aspect of life, I find myself very lucky to have supportive parents, especially my mother, who never made me realize the difference. I want to give every woman this experience, or at least try to make some difference in their life.

(2020)

In this interactive reading, you will learn more about Rukumani (Ruku) Tripathi and a group of midwives who are making a profound difference on health outcomes in Nepal. Reflective and conversation questions are included before and after each short section.

**Pre-reading:** What do you already know about Nepal?

Nepal, located in South Asia, is situated in the rugged and majestic Himalayan Mountain ranges. More than 70% of the county is covered by difficult mountain terrain. Although it borders both China and India, this geographic isolation, coupled with Nepal's historic political isolation, have made Nepal a unique country. Infrastructure is extremely limited in the country, contributing to challenges in health care and education. However, both health care and education have been expanding in recent years. The midwifery program at the National Academy of Medical Sciences is an important example of this critical expansion in both health care and education.

Nepal is a place of wonder. Its geography spans fertile plains, lush forests, and towering mountains, including Mount Everest. Nepal is home to an incredible variety of animal life, including tigers, leopards, wild ox, elephants, buffalo, wild sheep, snow leopards, wolves, and deer, and it is also one of the last homes for the giant Indian rhinoceros. An agricultural community, most Nepalese people work in tending, growing, and harvesting rice, corn, wheat, potatoes, sugarcane, and millet.

**Post-reading:** In these units, we have been exploring the land-body or land-health care connection. How do you think Nepal's geography and natural resources impact maternal health?

## Maternal Mortality Ratio in Nepal

**Pre-reading:** Why do you think the MMR might be difficult to calculate?

Maternal mortality is difficult to calculate. The World Health Organization reports that health information systems data in many low-income and under-resourced countries are often weak or unreliable and that even estimates from well-resourced systems suffer from misclassification. This leads to an underreporting of maternal deaths (World Health Organization, n.d.). For example, according to a research article from BioMed Central, from 2015 to 2020, the maternal death rate in Nepal was calculated at 129 per 100,000 births (Sitaula et al., 2021). However, the UNPFA calculates the MMR in Nepal at 239 in 100,000 live births (UNFPA, 2021).

Although the maternal death rate has fallen since the early 1990s, Nepal still has a high maternal mortality rate. As in most countries, many of these deaths are preventable. In fact, according to a study published in July 2021, "75% of those deaths [in Nepal] were preventable" (Sitaula et al., 2021).

> **Post-reading:** In these lessons, you keep learning that many maternal deaths are preventable. First, let's acknowledge what a heavy statement that is to read. What are the barriers and challenges to improving maternal health outcomes?

## Maternal Health and the COVID Pandemic

> **Pre-reading:** How did the COVID pandemic affect maternal health?

The COVID pandemic created many health challenges even beyond the coronavirus. In Nepal, when COVID-19 hit the country, the government told its citizens to stay at home and therefore, many people did not have access to critical prenatal and maternal health care. As a result, "258 women died of pregnancy or childbirth between March 2020 and June 2021" (*Nepal Sees Huge Rise in Maternal Deaths as Covid Keeps Women at Home*, 2021). Because expecting parents were not receiving the medical care they needed, a group of midwives, newly graduated from Nepal's first midwifery school, brainstormed a plan to help. These midwives first handed out their personal phone numbers and eventually created a toll-free telephone number for expecting parents to call to receive prenatal advice, referrals to local medical clinics, and mental health counseling. They provided information and counseling to more than 2,900 people, including pregnant women and lactating mothers (UNFPA, 2021).

Rukumani (Ruku) Tripathi is one of the midwives leading the initiatives to improve health outcomes for families in Nepal. She worked with her colleagues to create the toll-free number for Nepali citizens. In 2020, she was one of 100 outstanding women and nurse midwives who were honored for their heroic work and service to women (*100 Outstanding Women Nurse and Midwife Leaders*, 2020).

A recent study by Lancet Global Health cites midwives such as Ruku Tripathi as essential professionals in the work to improve maternal health outcomes. "Strengthening the capacity of midwives to deliver high-quality maternal and newborn health services has been highlighted as a priority by global health organisations" (Nove et al., 2021, para 1). This strategy has been especially transformative in LICs, such as Nepal. The UNFPA affirms this strategy and writes that "accelerating the number of professional midwives is key to reducing maternal deaths below 70 per 100,000 live births by 2030 in line with the Sustainable Development Goal target" (2021).

**Post-reading:**

◆ What other examples of extraordinary health work can you share from the COVID pandemic?
◆ How do you think Tripathi's knowledge as a Nepali woman increased her capacity to serve Nepali families? Be specific.

## Exit Questions

As a journal entry, reflect on the following questions.

◆ Is maternal health a justice issue? Why or why not?
◆ Is Rukumani (Ruku) Tripathi's story of the work of midwives in Nepal a story of radical hope? Defend your answer.

## Lesson 3: Inequities in Maternal Care—United States

| Term | Definition |
| --- | --- |
| Health disparities | Defined by the Centers for Disease Control and Prevention (CDC) as "preventable differences in the burden of disease, injury, violence, or opportunities to achieve optimal health that are experienced by socially disadvantaged populations" (2020). Health disparities are most pronounced among historically and currently marginalized groups of people, including communities of color, Indigenous communities, and members of the LGBTQIA+ community. |
| Structural racism | The systematic advantages and disadvantages that are embedded in institutions. These structural systems systematically disadvantage communities of color through the cumulative impacts of cultural, political, and historical forces. |
| Interpersonal racism | The biases that occur between individuals related to their beliefs about race, ethnicity, and country of origin. These biases can be deep-seated including beliefs about internalized oppression and internalized privilege, and they can present in overt and covert ways. |
| Disaggregated data | Data that are broken down into specific components (e.g. by race, ethnicity, zip code, or other discrete markers). This is contrasted with aggregated data, which put components together to summarize them. |

Racism—both interpersonal and structural—negatively affects the mental and physical health of millions of people, preventing them from attaining their highest level of health, and consequently, affecting the health of our nation. A growing body of research shows that centuries of racism in this country has had a profound and negative impact on communities of color. The impact is pervasive and deeply embedded in our society.

(Centers for Disease Control and Prevention [CDC], 2021)

While the United States has a significantly lower MMR than LICs, health disparities continue to be a pressing issue. In their 2020 report on racial disparities in maternal and infant health, Samantha Artiga, Olivia Pham, Kendal Orgera, and Usha Ranji report that "Despite continued advancements in medical care, rates of maternal mortality and morbidity and preterm birth have been rising in the U.S." (para 1). Both maternal and infant mortality rates are far higher in the United States than in other similarly large and wealthy countries. A 2017 study by National Public Radio and ProPublica reports that "More American women are dying of pregnancy-related complications than any other developed country. Only in the U.S. has the rate of women who die been rising" (Martin & Montagne, 2017a). Further, maternal health disparities map against racial lines with Black and Indigenous communities being at greatest risk for poor maternal and infant health outcomes (Artiga et al., 2020). Structural racism is a key barrier to maternal health as families of color are far more likely to die due to pregnancy- and childbirth-related complications than White families.

In this lesson, you will explore some of these health disparities and inequities, as well as potential supports and solutions. While these readings focus on health outcomes in the United States, it is important to highlight that many of the barriers discussed are present across our global community. The articles in this lesson highlight that racism, homophobia, transphobia, and health disparities persist among middle- and high-income countries, as well. They also give you the opportunity to practice radical hope as a form of resistance and advocacy.

## Article Jigsaw

There are three short readings below on maternal health disparities among Black, Indigenous, and LGBTQIA+ communities. They draw primarily on data from the United States. Working in small groups, read these articles and look for barriers and challenges as well as opportunities and solutions. After everyone has had a chance to read their article and reflect, educate others about your topic and share your insights.

### Reading 1: Health Disparities in Maternal Care: Black Women

In 2021, U.S. President Joe Biden and Vice President Kamala Harris declared April 11–17 Black Maternal Health Week. Declaring that "health care is a right" and that it is essential that "all women have equitable access to health care before, during, and after pregnancy," President Biden and Vice President Harris vowed to "amplify . . . the voices and experiences of Black women" to support their maternal health (The White House, 2021).

Although positive change is hopefully forthcoming, the following stories and statistics tell the story of a broken maternal health care system that needs to be overhauled to reverse traumatic and systemic disparities for Black mothers and their children.

Black women are three to four times more likely to die than White women during childbirth. As NPR notes, "Put another way, a black woman is . . . 243 percent more likely to die from pregnancy- or childbirth-related causes" than a White woman (Martin & Montagne, 2017b). Black mothers are also more likely to experience maternal health issues like postpartum depression and anxiety, and these numbers are even higher since these issues are often underreported.

There are many factors that contribute to illness, injury, and death before, during, and following childbirth. Black women are more likely to have untreated medical and mental health conditions than White women. Historical segregation and structural racism have created conditions in which Black families are less likely to have insurance or health benefits and more likely to give birth in hospitals with substandard care due to historical segregation. Black families are also more likely to experience racist stereotyping and may not feel respected, valued, or listened to within the healthcare system. Additionally, the chronic stress of multiple oppressions that are both raced and gendered takes its toll on maternal health (Martin & Montagne, 2017c).

In 2018, *The New York Times* ran a feature about the crisis of substandard care in the United States for Black women and their babies. The piece followed the story of Simone Landrum, a Black woman who lives in New Orleans. During her third pregnancy in 2016, she experienced high blood pressure; blinding headaches; and swelling in her hands, feet, and face. Her doctor, however, ignored both her high blood pressure and her symptoms and told her to take Tylenol. Eventually, she felt so bad that she went to the emergency room, where doctors discovered that her high blood pressure had caused her placenta to separate from her uterine wall. She nearly died, and tragically, her baby was stillborn. While Landrum went on to have another healthy baby, she again had to advocate for herself to dismissive health care workers to get the care she needed. This time, she had a birth doula who advocated for her as well (Villarosa, 2018).

Landrum's story is not an isolated case, and Black women across the United States experience an astonishingly tragic substandard level of care that affects their health and the health of their babies (*Black Mothers Respond to Our Cover Story on Maternal Mortality*, 2018). After publishing their article on substandard maternal care of Back women, *The New York Times* asked Black women to submit stories about their experiences with maternal care. They were flooded with hundreds of responses from Black women who had experienced being similarly dismissed by their medical team. The stories that *The New York Times* ran were from women who, even though their experiences were horrific and physically and emotionally damaging, survived pregnancy and childbirth. These are only one subset of stories from Black women in the United States. There are many more stories, as well; some of these are tragic and others are bright and full of hope. Across these stories is the continued need for more equitable maternal health care.

According to the CDC, "During 2016–2018, the pregnancy-related mortality ratios were:

◆ 41.4 deaths per 100,000 live births for non-Hispanic Black persons;
◆ 26.5 deaths per 100,000 live births for non-Hispanic American Indian or Alaska Native persons;
◆ 14.1 deaths per 100,000 live births for non-Hispanic Asian or Pacific Islander persons;
◆ 13.7 deaths per 100,000 live births for non-Hispanic White persons; and
◆ 11.2 deaths per 100,000 live births for Hispanic persons" (CDC, 2022).

**Let's Think Together**

◆ This is heavy and heartbreaking. Let's pause again to take an emotional temperature check. What do you need to better process this information? What surprised you the most in this article?
◆ Martin and Montagne found that the chronic stress of experiencing multiple intersecting oppressions including racism and sexism has a direct effect on maternal health. How might those stressors affect the health of mothers and babies?
◆ What is something about this topic that you would like to explore further? How can you best engage in that learning?

**Reading 2: Health Disparities in Maternal Care: Indigenous Women**

"Improving the health of Indigenous women and adolescent girls is achievable. It requires States to implement commitments to disaggregate data by ethnicity and age, tackle discrimination, and make health centers physically, financially, and culturally accessible" (UNPFA, 2018, para 3). Indigenous women face health disparities across the globe.

Work around this issue is needed in the United States as well. Currently, in the United States, Native American and Alaskan Native women die at a rate of two to three times higher than White mothers (Kozhimannil, 2020).

Dr. Katy B. Kozhimannil, a rural health researcher and Indigenous woman, writes:

Giving birth in the US is more deadly now than it was a generation ago. Deaths that occur during pregnancy, childbirth, or in the postpartum year are increasingly common. Maternal morbidity and mortality rates in the US highlight the fault lines of geography and race: people of color and rural residents face higher risks than their non-Hispanic White and urban counterparts.

(2020, p. 1)

Increased data, transparency, and stories from Indigenous women about their access to care and experiences with our health systems can help shift both narrative and practice. Researchers like Dr. Kozhimannil are bringing this issue into the light.

Stephanie Snook was an expecting mother who was pregnant with twins and had agreed to be interviewed for an NBC News story about the high rate of maternal deaths in Indigenous cultures in the United States. Tragically, 18 days before a scheduled cesarean section and before Snook could be interviewed, both she and her twins died. As Elizabeth Chuck and Haimy Assefa wrote in their piece on maternal health care in Indigenous cultures, "Snook was going to help shine a light on her race's troubling rate of maternal mortality. Instead, she became a statistic of it" (2020).

This is urgent work. Due to historical and current racism and oppression, Native American and Alaskan Native women in the United States are more likely to have undiagnosed medical conditions, are more likely to live in poverty, and are more likely to have limited access to care. Additionally, Native American and Alaskan Native women frequently navigate internalized oppression and racism, which can result "in chronic stress which can impact the life of a mother and whether or not she is able to carry her baby to full term" (NBC News, 2020, 5:42). The stress of internalized oppression and racism can affect the health of a pregnant mother and keep her from seeking care for the treatment she receives.

## Let's Think Together

- ◆ This is heavy and heartbreaking. Let's pause again to take an emotional temperature check. What do you need to better process this information? What surprised you the most in this article?
- ◆ Within the United States context, "approximately 60% of US maternal deaths are preventable" (Kozhimannil, 2020, p. 1). What are the primary barriers identified in this reading?
- ◆ What is something about this topic that you would like to explore further? How can you best engage in that learning?

## Reading 3: Health Disparities in Maternal Care: LGBTQIA+ Families

> Do yourself a favor as an ally and check your internalized homophobia. Don't be intrusive, don't ask questions that you wouldn't like to be asked about your life, don't assume anything, and be respectful. . . . Celebrate people's journey, focus on their resiliency and strengths, share the love.
>
> (dalidayblue, 2021)

Maternal health is not synonymous with "women's health." Transgender, gender non-conforming, and gender-fluid individuals who have a uterus can (and do) experience pregnancy. A 2019 study conducted by Family Equality found that 63% of queer and trans people between the ages of 18 and 35 were thinking about expanding their families, and birth is one way to do so. (Isaacs-Thomas, 2021).

When it comes to maternal health, disparities among the queer and trans community are often related to gendered systems; lack of affirming care; and misinformation, including the trauma of misgendering, more than they are related to medical complications. Brandt, MD, a maternal-fetal medicine specialist at Rutgers University in New Jersey, stated, "While pregnancy care for transgender patients and nonbinary individuals is not much more medically complex than the care of cisgender women, providers can focus on affirming their gender identities and addressing their social and emotional needs" (D'Ambrosio, 2022, para 5).

Although the data that is available suggests that an increasing number of LGBTQIA+ individuals are choosing to have babies, "Queer people's experiences of conception, pregnancy, birth and parenting are under-recorded, under-researched, and under-heard" (Darwin & Greenfield, 2019, p. 341).

Statistical analyses indicate that individuals in the LGBTQIA+ community may experience more miscarriage, stillborn babies, preterm births, and babies born with low birth weights than their heterosexual and cisgender counterparts (Everett et al., 2018). These may be related to chronic stress, marginalization, and discrimination. In addition, since some LGBTQIA+ people have children via surrogacy, artificial insemination, or adoption, the cost of having a baby can be an additional barrier to pregnancy and family making (Compton, 2018).

At the beginning of this unit, you read that families take many shapes—this diversity includes how individuals choose to expand their families to include infants and children. In addition to "mother" and "maternal," the *National Institute for Health Quarterly* has added more gender-neutral language to their care practices, including "birthing person/people." In their words, "at its core, inclusion is about creating more space for one another" (Brooks, 2021). Affirming health care, including maternal health and mental health, as universal human rights is aligned with UNs' SDG 3 on health and wellbeing.

**Let's Think Together**

◆ What surprised you in this article? How does this reading expand your understanding of maternal health and maternal health disparities among the LGBTQIA+ community?

◆ How might factors like gendered systems, lack of affirming care, and misinformation affect pregnancy care for LGBTQIA+ families?

◆ What is something about this topic that you would like to explore further? How can you best engage in that learning?

## Proposal Presentation

How do maternal health challenges affect your local community? Who are the advocates and changemakers working to improve maternal health in your community? How can you use your voice to bring about positive change? In this activity, you and your peers will explore these questions and develop a short three- to four-slide presentation proposal that could be presented at a local hospital to advocate for maternal health. As you are creating your proposal, consider the following:

◆ **Define *maternal health*:** What is the importance of quality, equitable maternal care?

◆ **Define the challenges:** What are the outcomes of poor maternal care? Draw on statistics and data for your local community, disaggregated by race and ethnic groups if possible.

◆ **Shine a light on solutions, advocacy, and knowledge:** What are the community resources and who are the local advocates engaged in this work? What do you want health care workers to know about structural racism, interpersonal racism, and sensitivity to cultural and religious practices around pregnancy and birth?

Consistent with our strengths-based work throughout this unit, remember the power of positive examples. For instance, you might seek an example of a hospital or birth center that has improved maternal care for families in marginalized communities and describe how they achieved better outcomes and how these ideas could be translated to more spaces.

# Concept Synthesis Activity—Impacting Change, Caring for My Community

Name _____ Date_____

In this unit, you learned about history makers, advocacy work toward gender justice, the sacred importance of land and water, and issues related to equitable maternal health. For this project, you and your peers will put our two focus terms into action by practicing *advocacy* and *mothering* as you address a pressing local issue with intentionality and care.

**STEP 1**—Working alone or in small groups, identify a local issue that you feel strongly about. Review your body of WGST work for inspiration. Below are a few suggestions:

- Climate change (see Unit 3, Lesson 3, pp. 80–85)
- Food insecurity (see Unit 4, Lessons 2–3, pp. 91–97)
- Access to clean water (see Unit 5, Lesson 4, pp. 131–35)
- Maternal health (see Unit 6, Lessons 1–3, pp. 138–154)
- Health disparities (See Unit 4, Lesson 2, pp. 91-94; Unit 6, Lesson 3, pp. 148–154)

| Topic: |
| --- |
| Select one issue you would like to focus on for this project. Choose an issue that you are interested in, one that has a strong local connection, and one in which you believe you could implement an achievable action plan. |
|  |

**STEP 2**—Connect this work to the UNs' SDG 5, which is to "Achieve gender equality and empower all women and girls." (You can refer back to your research work in Unit 1, Lesson 1, pp. 25–28.) Some of the targets of SDG 5 are:

- Expand equality and end discrimination.
  - End discrimination against women and girls (5.1).

- Adopt and strengthen policies and enforceable legislation for gender equality (5.C).

◆ Expand reproductive health and end violence.

- End all violence and exploitation against women and girls (5.2).
- Eliminate forced and child marriages (5.3).
- Universal access to reproductive rights and health (5.6).

◆ Create equal leadership and economic opportunities.

- Ensure full participation in leadership and decision-making (5.5).
- Equal rights to economic resources, property ownership, and financial services (5.A).

◆ Expand mobility and value domestic work.

- Promote empowerment of women through technology (5.B).
- Value unpaid care and promote shared domestic responsibilities (5.4).

| **Research:** |
| --- |
| How does this issue connect to SDG 5? |
|  |

**STEP 3**—Develop a plan to make an impact. Before developing your action plan, review the section on radical hope in research (pp. 140–43). The ways we approach research and action matter. Draw on the wisdom of community leaders (including youth leaders) and serve as a humble learner. Identify a specific need and develop an action plan you and your peers can implement in a month. Change is often incremental. While you and your peers won't dismantle structural racism or solve housing insecurity with this project, you can still make an important difference on issues of justice, equity, and humanity. Remember that one project can lead to another and another and so on.

**Get Specific on Need:**

What is the specific need you want to address? What resources can you access to help address this need (people, materials, etc.)?

**Get Specific in Planning:**

What steps will you need to take to accomplish this project? Think in terms of beginning, middle, and end. What will you need to do first? How will you spread the word about your campaign or project? How will you know if your project is successful?

**STEP 4**—Reflect. Following your project, reflect on the following questions. This step should be completed individually.

1. What am I most proud of about this action project?
2. What is something I would do differently next time?
3. What is the most powerful thing I learned about the issue that I chose and how it relates to SDG 5?
4. How will I continue this important work?

## Extension Exercises for Concept 3

### Allowables—Metaphors That Matter

Nikki Giovanni (1943–) once said, "I come from a long line of storytellers" (Poetry Foundation, n.d.), and that heritage is evident in her writing as a poet who tells her story and in her work as an educator and activist who helps other people tell their stories. Her writing is political, powerful, intimate, intersectional, and accessible. Giovanni is the recipient of many awards, including The Rosa Parks Woman of Courage Award and the Caldecott Honor Book Award, and she was a Grammy nominee for Best Spoken Word Album.

Giovanni's poem "Allowables" has been used as an analogy for police brutality against African Americans. This poem would pair well with our discussions around modern abolitionist work (Unit 2, Lesson 1). Read this short poignant poem together and discuss how poetry can be used for social change. A link to the poem is located in this lesson's appendix. Challenge scholars to utilize metaphor, like Giovanni, as they author original poems on social issues that matter to them.

### History Maker—Stacey Abrams

Stacey Abrams, a lawyer and voting rights activist, said, "Effective leaders must be truth seekers and that requires a willingness to understand truths other than our own" (2018, p. 170). Abrams is truly one of today's history makers. She is responsible for mobilizing 800,000 people to register to vote in her home state of Georgia in advance of the 2020 elections.

Explore the TED Radio Interview with Stacey Abrams. This 25-minute podcast is framed around her identity as a student and contains powerful messages for scholars and student leaders.

You might spread the listening out over four days. This will give you and your class about 5–8 minutes per day or roughly one big question. Reporter Manoush Zomorodi's questions and Stacey Abrams' stories point to purposeful reflection and personal connection. After listening to each short segment, give scholars space to process, make connections, and discuss. Try a different processing method each day, including free writing, Socratic seminar discussions, and whole-group dialogue. Close the week with a whole class discussion of key takeaways from Abrams' interview, any new intentions scholars want to set, and a list for future research questions.

◆ Explore Abrams' run for governor in the state of Georgia followed by her subsequent work around voting rights. What advocacy lessons can we learn from her work?

◆ Research the history of voting rights, voting suppression, and voter mobilization in the United States. How does the U.S. voting process compare to other countries?

## Guest Experts in Maternal Health

Connect with a midwife, doula, OBGYN, OBGYN nurse, or group working on maternal health in your community. Invite these experts to your classroom either as individual presenters or as a panel. Panel conversations often lead to new synergies and complexities of ideas. Building on these connections, learn more about maternal health needs in your own community, and explore ways to make a difference. Relationships such as these sometimes lead to service projects, field trips, or educational outreach initiatives.

## History Maker—Dr. Shalon's Maternal Action Project

Dr. Shalon Irving held dual PhDs in sociology and gerontology and two master's degrees, including one in public health. She was an epidemiologist at the CDC, where she focused on community health, equity, and transparency in health care. Drawing on her own lived experiences as a Black woman, Dr. Irving wanted to expand equity and eradicate racism in our health care systems.

As she stated on her Twitter bio, "I see inequity wherever it exists, call it by name, and work to eliminate it. I vow to create a better earth!" (Irving, n.d.). Tragically, three weeks after this tweet, she gave birth to a baby girl and then died of complications due to high blood pressure. Dr. Irving had frequently brought concerns about her health to her doctor.

After Dr. Irving's death, her mother, Wanda Irving, began speaking about maternal health and race equity and also began a nonprofit called Dr. Shalon's Maternal Action Project which seeks to expose racial inequity in maternal care for African American women, develop strategies to improve maternal care, and provide a space where Black women can tell their stories and receive support (*Convention on the Elimination of All Forms of Discrimination against Women*, n.d.). Dr. Shalon's Maternal Action Project takes a multi-faceted approach to advocacy work.

According to their website, "We believe change needs to happen at national and institutional levels, supported by leaders in politics and health-care. But we also believe that the most powerful tool a Black mother has is her voice." The four pillars of action for Dr. Shalon's Maternal Action Project are storytelling, empowerment, community building, and education.

◆ Dr. Shalon's Maternal Action Project emphasizes the importance of storytelling and states that "the most powerful tool a black mother has is her voice." Why is storytelling important to the work of improving maternal health and reducing health disparities?

◆ According to the CDC, epidemiologists are like "disease detectives." They "search for the cause of disease, identify people who are at risk, determine how to control or stop the spread or prevent it from happening again" (n.d.). How do you think an epidemiologist can help expand equity in our health care systems?

◆ Dr. Irving focused her education and skills as an epidemiologist to help eliminate inequity. Think about the type of job you want to have. What are some ways you might use that job to improve equity?

## Helpful Links

Ms Magazine's *Tribute to Harriet Tubman*

◆ https://msmagazine.com/tubman200/?fbclid=IwAR3K-CYV8IDEoLSswuFkN7DvzfrP1-z-rY7NHtzjKtnSGVRiJeYj8o0SddTY

*The Women of the Women's March*

◆ www.wmagazine.com/story/womens-march-on-washington-activists-organizers

*Interview with Stacey Abrams*

◆ www.npr.org/2021/01/06/953980644/bonus-episode-stacey-abrams

*News Articles Toward a More Complete Teaching of the 19th Amendment*

◆ "The U.S. suffragette movement tried to leave out Black women. They showed up anyhow" (*The Guardian*)
◆ "How early suffragist left black Women out of their fight" (history)
◆ "How history classes on the women's suffrage movement leave out the work of Black voting rights activists"
◆ "Unlearning history: The woman's suffrage movement" (PBS)

*Equal Rights Amendment*

◆ Short teaching video on the ERA and why we need its protection: www.youtube.com/watch?v=Tjnk3zBo-1I

*Nikki Giovanni's "Allowables" Transcript*

◆ https://artistic.umn.edu/allowables-poem-nikki-giovanni

*Women and Standing Rock*

- ◆ This resource includes "Prayer of prayers: For the water protectors at standing rock," by Deborah Miranda: https://orionmagazine.org/article/women-standing-rock/

## Notes

[1] To *expunge* means to erase or remove completely.

[2] Note: you will explore more art methods in the proseminar. Therefore, you may want to come back to this project with new ideas after completing that lesson series.

[3] As of the publication of this book, the amendment still needed more congressional sponsors to move forward.

[4] The Water Protectors at Standing Rock began as a small group of activists that expanded into thousands of demonstrators who were protesting against the nearly 1,200-mile Dakota Access Pipeline that was being built across the Missouri River and through sacred land belonging to the Standing Rock Sioux people (Research Guides: The Dakota Access Pipeline: Native American Perspectives: Home, 2020).

[5] In addition to the direct impact improved maternal health has across communities, this unit also celebrates that birth stories can take many shapes. On pp. 153–54 there is a reading on maternal health care with a focus on LGBTQIA+ families that specifically discusses care for trans and gender non-conforming parents.

# Proseminar: Artivism

## Foreword by Stefani Domingues, Advisory Editor

*Stefani Domingues (she/her) is 28 years old and is a proud Latina, feminist, educator, and youth mobilizer. She holds a bachelor's degree in psychology and currently serves as clinical psychologist for adolescents and young women. Prior to that, she worked for five years serving middle and high school students who were pursuing international education. Stefani believes that young girls can gain confidence by relating to strong and talented women who came before them. In her free time, she enjoys reading novels. Her favorite author is the Brazilian writer Clarice Lispector. As a personal dream, Stefani wishes to someday publish her own novel featuring a bold feminine protagonist.*

Sou orgulhosamente latina, feminista, educadora e mobilizadora de joventudes. Nos últimos 5 anos, trabalhei com educação internacional para alunas e alunos do Ensino Fundamental e Médio. Atualmente atuo como psicóloga clínica de meninas e mulheres jovens. Na prática clínica, juntas, construímos um ambiente seguro para compartilhar lutas, sucessos e criar modos de usar as emoções de forma poderosa e transformadora.

Durante minha adolescência, me vi procurando em todos os lugares por representação e inspiração femininas. Não foi até recentemente que eu entendi

DOI: 10.4324/9781003323327-5

o porquê de precisar procurar tanto. Percebi que era mais difícil me imaginar em lugares protagonistas simplesmente porque não estava acostumada a ver mulheres em cargos de liderança, ou ter sua arte celebrada em galerias, ou viver uma história que não fosse sobretudo sobre casamento ou maternidade. As formas como as mulheres são representadas ou não são importantes para mim e para as jovens com quem trabalho. Ao ver apenas uma história ou uma versão dela, parecia que o casamento e a maternidade não eram escolhas, mas a única conquista pela qual eu deveria me esforçar ou me orgulhar. Eu buscava ansiosamente por uma maior representação de gênero e só conseguia encontrá-la quando procurava ativamente por isso.

Exatamente por isso que este livro, *Teaching Women's and Gender Studies*, é tão importante. Ele propõe preencher uma lacuna e engajar as gerações mais jovens na construção de uma sociedade mais justa. A fim de capacitar os jovens e alcançar equidade de gênero, alunas e alunos precisam ser intencionalmente introduzidos aos estudos de gênero e teorias feministas.

Cada um de nós lê a partir de seu próprio contexto e experiências vividas. Enquanto trabalhava com Kathryn e Jill neste capítulo, muitas vezes pensei na cantora brasileira Elza Soares (1930–2022) que cantou "*minha voz uso pra dizer o que se cala.*" Nascida no Brasil, sua voz foi um instrumento de resistência que inspirou a muitas, inclusive a mim. Sua arte explorou a violência e as desigualdades que a acompanharam ao longo de sua vida; no entanto, ao ouvir suas músicas, você também pode ouvir sua alegria, raiva e criatividade.

Kathryn e Jill afetivamente conduzem estudantes e educadores por uma exposição de pintoras, escritoras e poetizas engajadas no trabalho feminista. Essas obras e diversos exemplos podem inspirar a juventude a entender como as artes podem levar à transformação. Professores, estudantes e educadores encontrarão recursos poderosos para promover discussões importantes em sala de aula. Conhecerão também mulheres de destaque, artistas pretas e latinas que impactaram suas comunidades. Através deste trabalho, você e suas salas de aula também podem resistir à injustiça e encontrar uma esperança radical.

I am a proud Latina, feminist, educator, and youth mobilizer. For the past five years, I've worked with international education for middle and high school students. Currently I serve as a clinical psychologist for girls and young women. In private practice, together, we build a safe environment to share struggles and successes and create ways to use our emotions in a powerful and transformative way.

Growing up, I found myself looking everywhere for women's representation and inspiration. It was not until recently that I understood why. I realized that it was harder for me to picture myself in protagonistic places simply because I was not used to seeing women in leadership positions, or having their art celebrated in galleries, or living a story that was not primarily about marriage or motherhood. The ways women are represented or not represented mattered to me, and it matters to the young people I work with. By only seeing one story or one version of a story, it seemed that marriage and motherhood were not choices, but the only achievement I should strive for or be proud of. I was eager for greater gender representation, and I could only find it when I was actively looking for it.

That is why this resource, *Teaching Women's and Gender Studies*, is so important. It proposes to fill a gap and engage young generations in building a more equitable society. To empower young people and achieve gender justice, students need to be intentionally introduced to gender studies and feminist theories.

Each of us reads from our own context and lived experiences. As I was working with Kathryn and Jill on this section, I often thought of the Brazilian singer Elza Soares (1930–2022). She sang that *"minha voz eu uso pra dizer o que se cala."*[1] Growing up in Brazil, her voice was an instrument for resistance that inspired my peers and me. Her art explored the violence and inequalities that accompany her throughout her life; however, when listening to her songs you can also hear joy, anger, and creativity.

Kathryn and Jill affectionately walk scholars and educators through an exhibition of painters, writers, and poets engaged in feminist work. These works and diverse examples can inspire youth to see how the arts can lead to transformation. Teachers, scholars, and educators will find powerful resources to promote important discussions in the classroom. They will also meet outstanding women, particularly women of color, who have impacted their communities. Through this work, you and your class communities can seek ways to resist injustice and find radical hope.

---

**Teaching Notes**

**A proseminar** is typically a course that is based on readings and dialogue around a specific topic. These courses are usually offered in graduate school but open to advanced undergraduate students. We (Kathryn and Jill) included a proseminar in this book to offer you the opportunity to give scholars extended experiences in a new topic in WGST—*artivism*.

You might teach this proseminar to your entire class/es or offer it as an enrichment seminar to a small group before or after school. You will find a close reading protocol for analyzing images on p. 167–68. Reading images may be a new skill for some of the scholars in your classes, and this protocol helps walk scholars through a sophisticated analysis. Several advanced placement courses ask scholars to engage in similar analyses and reads of images.

Our hope is that these activities expose scholars to exciting art and activist projects while building on their earlier WGST lessons and preparing them for future studies and leadership work.

The final proseminar project is an art making project where scholars work either independently or in small teams to create a work inspired by some of the feminist works they study. We recommend hosting a public gallery of the final pieces in which scholars can share about their art making and the connections they made to their studies throughout the earlier lessons and their proseminar content.

 **Thought Questions**
- When is art a form of resistance?
- How are art and justice related?
- How can you use your passions, talents, and creativity for social good?

Throughout these units, you have explored and celebrated the creative ways activists are expanding access, telling more complete stories, and working toward greater gender justice. In this proseminar, you will meet activists and *artivists* who are using their creative talents for social good. Artivism has the potential to challenge racism, sexism, discrimination, and injustice; to raise awareness about inequities and injustice; and to help viewers imagine and work intentionally toward a more just reality. Artists from all over the world are exploring the combination of creativity and activism to challenge inequities and create a new narrative. In Brazil, for example, artivists from Rio de Janeiro's poorest communities, the *favelas*, are helping to rewrite a new narrative about race, class, and gender. Carmen Martinez and Kerry Carrington (2021) studied art movements from the favelas and said that these works create a "paradigm of potential . . . and give visibility to another periphery which affirms itself through its agency, inventiveness, and nonviolent pathways." In particular, they cite *passinho*[2] dancers and slam poets as creators who are actively challenging patriarchy, racism, and heteronormativity through their art.

| Term | Definition |
|---|---|
| Artivism | A combination of art and activism, whereby artists address injustice, inequities, and other social challenges through creative expression. Artivists aim to increase awareness of social issues and reimagine and reclaim new possibilities through their work. Artivists may use a variety of mediums including slam poetry, music, dance, mural, performance art, large-scale installations, and graphic design. |
| Feminist Art Movement | An expansive multi-media arts movement that sought to (1) provide greater gender representation in art, (2) correct for and expose the erasure of women's stories and full identities, (3) and resist the reproduction of gender stereotypes in art (Rise Art, 2021). |

## Close Reading for Art Images

The civil rights and social justice movements of the mid-late 1960s contributed to what is now called the *Feminist Art Movement*. Artists and activists during this period

> sought to rewrite a falsely male-dominated art history, change the contemporary world around them through their art, intervene in the established art world, and challenge the existing art canon. Feminist Art created opportunities and spaces that previously did not exist for women and minority artists.
>
> (The Art Story, n.d., para 1)

In this proseminar activity, engage in a close read of one of the following feminist art images.

## Art Pieces for a Close Read

- ◆ Emma Amos—*Preparing for a Face Lift*
- ◆ Miriam Schapiro—*Costume for Mother Earth*
- ◆ *MaestraPeace*—San Francisco Women's Mural (Juana Alicia, Miranda Bergman, Edythe Boone, Susan Kelk Cervantes, Meera Desai, Yvonne Littleton, and Irene Perez)

Name _____ Date _____

## Close Reading for Images—A Viewing Protocol

Title _____
Artist _____

| | |
|---|---|
| **First Read**<br>This step is similar to how you might skim a nonfiction work before diving in. Take a moment to take in the piece. What stands out to you or calls your attention? Does the piece invite you in and appeal to your sensibilities? Is it a piece that will require more intentionally to wrestle with? | |
| **Color and Light**<br>How does the artist use color and light? Are the colors bright and vivid or muted and understated? Where are the brightest brights and darkest darks? Are the colors and use of light realistic or exaggerated? How do these choices contribute to the overall tone of the art piece? | |
| **Texture and Line**<br>How is texture and line used in this piece? Is this piece realistic? Abstract? Exaggerated? If so, how? What textures or lines catch your eye? Does the piece seem flat and two-dimensional or more curved and three-dimensional? How do these choices contribute to the overall tone of the piece? | |
| **Space and Movement**<br>How do your eyes move along the piece? What design choices has the artist made to help tell their story? How are they using negative and positive space in this piece? How do the different elements in this piece work together and/or work separately? | |

| | | | |
|---|---|---|---|
| **Emotion and Message**<br>What message do you think the artist was trying to make with this piece? How does this image make you feel? What does this image make you think of? Are there spaces that surprise you or moments where the artist has clearly taken a risk? | | | |
| **Context**<br>When was the piece created and for what purpose? What do you know about the artist? How does this background information influence your reading of the piece? | | | |
| **Connection**<br>How does this piece connect to other art you have analyzed? How does this piece connect to current events or literature you have studied? Finally, how is this piece in conversation or conflict with your own lived experiences? | | | |
| **Critical Thinking Response**<br>Just as with literature, your lived experiences and reading of this piece matter in how you interpret it. Review your notes in this table. Write a few summarizing sentences on the strategies the artist used to convey their message or create this piece and any key connections you made to this piece or the artist's overall message. | | | |

## Artivism Case Studies

Next, explore three case studies of artivists who are using art to address inequities, challenge limited definitions, and invite new possibilities. Each case study includes an extension activity.

**Case Study 1: Shamsia Hassani—Street Art as Resistance (Afghanistan)**

**"Art changes people's minds and people change the world,"** writes Shamsia Hassani, who has gained acclaim and attention as Afghanistan's first woman street artist.

Street artists, also sometimes known as graffiti artists or public artists, are an incredibly diverse group, and many street artists come from identity backgrounds that experience discrimination, exclusion, silencing, and violence. The *Harvard Political Review* (2020) writes, "If you are a street artist, there's a higher chance of you being low-income, a person of color, female, or part of the LGBTQIA+ community" (Choi, 2020, para 6). In addition to challenging whom art is for, street art also challenges what spaces count as art spaces. Street art represents expansive thinking about the form and function of art. It is often a reclaiming of voice or story, as well as an act of resistance that would silence those stories. These themes color Hassani's work, as well.

According to her website (2021), Hassani's art

> gives Afghan women a different face, a face with power, ambitions, and willingness to achieve goals. The woman character used in her artworks portrays a human being who is proud, loud, and can bring positive changes to people's lives. During the last decade of postwar era in Afghanistan, Shamsia's works have brought in a huge wave of color and appreciation to all the women in the country.
>
> (para 2)

- ◆ What do you know about street art, and what would you like to learn about street art?
- ◆ Do you know any street artists?
- ◆ Are street art and mural work the same or different? How so?
- ◆ How does the street art media contribute to our themes of resistance, representation, and radical hope?

**Extension Activity**—Shamsia Hassani offers an extensive collection of her artwork for viewing on her website. Visit her exhibition collection linked at the end of this chapter. Choose an exhibit or two, and spend some time exploring her art. As you do, use our close viewing protocol (p. 167–68) and discuss one question per image.

### Case Study 2: Las Krudas (Cuba and the United States)

In 1996, Odaymara Cueta, Olivia "Oli" Prendes, and Oadlys Cuesta founded the first vegan and queer activist arts group in Havana, Cuba, called Cubensi. Their art expanded who hip hop was for and what hip hop could do. Their music centered "the social and economic reality of being Black and female in Cuba" (Armstead, 2007, p. 109), and their work has continued to expand to include trans and queer rights and continued gender justice work. In addition to performing, the group has strong roots in teaching and has brought music and theater to children in Cuba.

In 2006, Odaymara Cuesta and Oli Prendes immigrated to Texas in the United States and rebranded as Las Krudas. The duo self-identifies on their Krudas Cubensi website as "fat, feminist, queer, trans non-binary, black & brown vegan immigrants [who] are aware that most of these intersections are underrated in the music industry" (Krudas Cubensi, n.d.). Their lyrics address the intersectionalities of gender, race, class, power, and sexual orientation and challenge systems of discrimination and exploitation. Using music as an act of resistance against oppression, they celebrate and affirm a vibrant range of identities. The duo continues to perform and hold workshops across North and South American and the Caribbean (Archwy, 2021). The Kennedy Center (n.d.), one of the most acclaimed performing centers in the United States, writes that Las Krudas represents "womyn, immigrants, queer and people of color action as a central part of world change."

### ⏵ Extension Activity

View the Las Krudas music video "La Gorda," which is linked in the section appendix. How does this connect to our conversations about beauty, gender, power, and representation?

### Case Study 3: Christine ("CK") Sun Kim—Sound Artist (United States)

Christine ("CK") Sun Kim (1980–), the daughter of Korean immigrant parents, is an American sound artist based in Berlin. She uses drawing, performance, and video to explore how sound functions in society. Her unique and rich perspective to this theme is informed by her identity as a Deaf person. Much like other artists who have remarked that their art or identity is political, Kim says being a Deaf person is political. "I constantly questioned the ownership of sound," Kim says, "now I'm reclaiming sound as my property" (Artsy, n.d., para 1).

Deaf people continue to face discrimination, erasure, and injustice in both overt and covert ways. For example, Deaf people are often unemployed or underemployed, and Deaf women are six times more likely to be sexually assaulted than hearing women (The World, 2020). They also face a myriad of microaggressions, including being ignored, excluded, patronized, and bullied. Kim tackles these injustices headfirst in works such as *Deaf Rage* and *Trauma, LOL* using pie charts and graphs to diagram her lived experiences and illustrate the obtuse, acute, and legit (right angle) rage she experiences navigating an injustice and often inaccessible world.

**Extension Activity**—View Christine Sun Kim's TED Talk on "The Enchanting Music of Sign Language" and then respond to the following questions.

- ◆ Why is "p" Kim's favorite musical annotation?
- ◆ What role does sound play in her life? What unique wisdom or perspective does she bring to understanding sound?

Kim shares,

> So I decided to reclaim ownership of sound and to put it into my art practice. And everything that I had been taught regarding sound, I decided to do away with and unlearn. I started creating a new body of work. And when I presented this to the art community, I was blown away with the amount of support and attention I received.
>
> (4:56)

- ◆ What is something you would like to unlearn or reclaim and why?

# Proseminar Project

**Name** _____ **Date**_____

During this unit, you have explored art and artivism from around the world. Choose one (or more) of these pieces from our proseminar study as inspiration for creating your own work. Your piece should illustrate one or more of our course themes: *representation, resistance,* and *radical hope.* As you plan your piece, consider the presence of joy and/or anger in the message or story you are telling. All media, including mixed media and performance, are welcome. You may work independently or in a collaborative group. If you are working in chalk or engaged in performance art, please also take images or video of your final piece.

Tip: Refer to *the Close Reading Protocol* for elements to consider in your own work.

## Artist Statement

Each artist will submit an individual artist statement about their piece. Below is some guidance for your artist statement.

| | |
|---|---|
| Title | What is the title of this work? What is the meaning of the title? |
| Thesis | What is the main message of your piece? What do you want viewers to learn or experience when they read your work? |
| Lived experiences | How does this piece connect to you and your peers' lived experiences? What does the viewer learn about you in reading this work? How is joy and/or anger present in this piece? |
| Course theme(s) | How does your piece illustrate or show a commitment to resistance, representation, or radical hope? Be specific. |
| Inspiration | Give a brief background on the artist(s) who inspired you. This may also be a good place to discuss the materials you chose to use in creating your art and why you chose those materials or media. |
| Scholarly connections | Building on your WGST body of research and work, connect your art project to at least four other sources, theories, or themes from our studies. |

**Helpful Links**

- *Preparing for a Facelift* Emma Amos: https://journal.alabamachanin.com/2020/07/thosewhoinspireus-emma-amos/
- On Miriam Schapiro, Femmage Morning Edition: www.wnyc.org/story/review-miriam-schapiro-soon/
- Emma Amos—Georgia Museum of Art: https://georgiamuseum.org/exhibit/emma-amos-color-odyssey/
- Shamsia Hassani's website: www.shamsiahassani.net/
- Shamsia Hassani's Exhibitions: www.shamsiahassani.net/exhibitions
- Christine Sun Kim's "The Enchanting Music of ASL": www.ted.com/talks/christine_sun_kim_the_enchanting_music_of_sign_language?language=en
- Christine Sun Kim's *The World is Sound*, "Sound of . . ." series: www.youtube.com/watch?v=3vU4TCKxZlc
- Las Krudas "La Gorda": www.youtube.com/watch?v=Mlzf9BPHZYo

## Notes

[1] Translated from Portuguese: *My voice I use to speak about what is silent*.

[2] Passinho is a dance that originated in the favelas and gained international acclaim following the 2016 Olympics. It has been cited as a dance form that has helped challenge race and gender norms and contribute to border crossing and bridge building between cultures.

# Epilogue

## By Advisory Editor Lisa DeCastro

*Lisa DeCastro (she/her) currently serves as the elementary coordinator at Mizzou Academy. She has had the privilege of learning and laughing with kindergarten and first grade students and believes in the value of all student voices, especially those of our youngest learners. Lisa lives in California with her husband, two sons, and beloved four-legged Weimaraner, Gunther. As the only woman in her family, one of her most important jobs is raising kind and compassionate sons. Her perfect day begins with a brisk morning walk, watering her plants, and sitting in her backyard, coffee in hand, and reading the newspaper.*

One of my earliest memories from school is reading to my classmates in the library nook of Miss O'Brien's first grade classroom. The book I chose was *Lisa and Lynn* by Dick Bruna. I have no recollection of what the simple story was about other than this was my favorite book because *my* name was on the front cover. It didn't matter that the character, Lisa, with blonde pigtails and fair skin, looked nothing like me. I was a girl, had pigtails, but they were black—we shared the same name, and that was enough for me. With pride, I sat in the rocking chair and read *Lisa and Lynn* to my classmates sitting on the rug in front of me.

When I reflect on this memory, so many questions percolate in my mind. I yearn to ask my six-year-old self: *Do you remember any books that featured girls*

DOI: 10.4324/9781003323327-6

*that looked like you or represented your Filipino-American family?* Did I notice that all of the books and stories I read as a child, and even into my teens, had no characters that looked like me, my brother, or my family? To make my family even more unique, my family was intergenerational—my grandmother lived with us, and my mother worked full-time which was remarkably different from any family of my friends or in the neighborhood. Where were the books that told a story similar to mine?

In this closing section of *Teaching Women's and Gender Studies*, Kathryn and Jill have inspired teachers and students to walk boldly and bravely on a journey to advance diversity, inclusion, and representation in their school communities. Today there are an increasing number of children's books that depict more diverse characters and are also written by more authors of color. As an adult, when I discovered the children's book *Cora Cooks Pancit* by Dora K. Lazo Gilmore, my heart swelled with both pride and the feeling of "it's about time" for a book with characters who represent my childhood self and family. As educators, it is imperative that our students see themselves in the curriculum, books, and resources that we carefully choose to bring into our classrooms. Even in the years that have passed since being in the classroom, I have noticed there are a number of picture books that celebrate children and families with multicultural and diverse perspectives. Imagine schools with classroom libraries full of books that represent the tapestry of our multidimensional students. How would their identities be shaped when validated and represented? How would the self-confidence of neurodivergent students grow and blossom? How does that impact students' beliefs and actions toward inclusion? What message does it send?

Jill and Kathryn call upon us to continue affirming our students and to expand the affirmations to celebrations of gender and (dis)abilities. We know as adults and lifelong learners that students build their confidence within themselves and others, take risks, and stand up for their beliefs when they are in a safe place and surrounded by caring and compassionate people. My own evolution as a teacher began by switching "Good morning, boy and girls" to "Good morning, friends." More recently, I have been adding my pronouns to my name wherever I can and using terms such as "Latinx" to promote gender inclusion. These intentional choices that we make with our words may seem small but can yield many positives for humanity and compassion.

Our schools can be places of change, revolution, and inclusion when we embrace the growth that may stem from discomfort. Classroom discussions about representation and equity for LGBTQIA+ and disability communities can be unpredictable. Sharing feelings about gender identities and sexuality can be uncomfortable for students who are new to discussion of such topics. As teachers, we can model and show our students how to risk feelings of vulnerability and truths that may not have surfaced for us before, and we may not have the answers to where to put all these emotions. *Teaching Women's and Gender Studies* gives educators the place to start because they matter to those whose stories have not been shared or listened to yet. This important work is rooted in justice, equity, and inclusion and cannot be done alone. Seek out and form partnerships to collaborate with other teachers at your school.

A few years ago, I had the opportunity to attend teacher leadership training where one session focused on a basic principle of improv comedy, "yes, and." The "yes" accepts the truth. The "and" determines the response and the desire to move forward. Imagine the power of "yes, and" when used to affirm differences and (dis)abilities as strengths, overcome challenges, and foster inclusion. I can hear Arianna in second grade saying, "Yes I have ADHD, and I keep trying to draw this monarch butterfly," or William, a high school sophomore saying, "Yes, I have dyslexia, and I will reread this chapter after school with my teacher." Throughout this book, Jill and Kathryn set the stage for teachers and students to embrace *"yes, and"* while embarking on a journey to discover and celebrate the power that comes from within each other and their communities. With tenacity in our hearts and standing on the shoulders of each other, we must keep looking for the light shining in the rainbows of radical hope. As Arundhati Roy (2004), the writer and activist, reminded us, "Another world is not only possible, she is on her way. On a quiet day, I can hear her breathing" (p. 86).

# Glossary

| Term | Definition | Unit |
|------|------------|------|
| Abolition | The ending of a practice, system, or institution, often in reference to institutional racism or the systematic denial of human rights such as human enslavement. | 5 |
| Advocacy | The act of supporting and working toward a specific cause, which can include organizing, educating, lobbying, training, and mobilizing. | 2 |
| Allyship | The active and intentional practice of being for a person or group of people to which you do not belong. Generally, allyship is when a person with more privilege or power in a specific area acts for or on behalf of those who are systematically marginalized or disempowered in that area. Allies continue to take action even when they are unsure of the outcome and/or when acting on behalf of this group carries personal risk. Allyship is about justice and not personal gain. | 2 |
| Artivism | A combination of art and activism, whereby artists address injustice, inequities, and other social challenges through creative expression. Artivists aim to increase awareness of social issues and reimagine and reclaim new possibilities through their work. Artivists may use a variety of media, including slam poetry, music, dance, mural, performance art, large-scale installations, and graphic design. | Proseminar |

| Binary | Consisting of only two parts (related: binary thinking or believing there are only two parts) | 1 |
|---|---|---|
| Black feminisms | This framework centers the experiences of Black women while exploring the ways multiple identities and oppressions intersect to create contextualized experiences and conditions within systems. Black feminisms work concurrently on eradicating racism and sexism in the work toward a more just world. (See especially Sojourner Truth, Kimberlé Crenshaw, Angela Davis, and bell hooks.) | 2 |
| Center | A concept to help us think about social space. The center can be a philosophical or physical space (noun); however, *to center* can also be a verb meaning to be seen, heard, known, and celebrated. | 3 |
| Cisgender | People whose gender aligns with the sex they were assigned at birth. For example, if a baby was assigned male at birth and identifies as a boy/man, he would be considered cisgender (or cis). | 1 |
| Climate justice | A movement that acknowledges how climate change affects people in marginalized communities in disproportional and exponential ways. This movement then advocates for these inequalities to be addressed and for solutions to be implemented. | 4 |
| Colonization | To violently establish control over the Indigenous people of an area. This control is intended to benefit those coming to the land and colonizing, even at the great harm of those who have previously cared for and called the land home. In addition to physical harm, Indigenous traditions and culture are often devalued or destroyed during colonization. | 1 |

| Critical consciousness | An ability to see and understand inequities in our communities and a commitment to take action against injustices. | 2 |
|---|---|---|
| Disaggregated data | Data that are broken down into specific components (e.g. by race, ethnicity, zip code, or other discrete markers). This is contrasted with aggregated data, which put components together to summarize them. | 6 |
| Eurocentrism | Excluding or omitting the multiple global perspectives, experiences, cultures, and histories that make our world and casting European culture and history as the norm. | 3 |
| Equality | Having the same status, rights, and opportunities. | 1 |
| Equity | Fairness and justice; equity is different from equality (see equality) in that it recognizes that different people have different experiences, opportunities, access, and needs. Because of this, equity work requires systematic change to remove barriers, adjust imbalances, and create more just solutions and systems. | 1 |
| Feminism | An affirmation of humanity that seeks freedom from oppression and commits to the full access of social, health, economic, and political rights and opportunities for all people. (See also the definitions and discussion of Black feminisms, transnational and global feminisms, queer theory, liberal feminisms, and radical feminisms.) | 1 |
| Feminist Art Movement | An expansive multi-media arts movement that sought to (1) provide greater gender representation in art, (2) correct for and expose the erasure of women's stories and full identities, (3) and resist the reproduction of gender stereotypes in art (Rise Art, 2021). | Proseminar |

| Food insecurity | Defined by the Food and Agricultural Organization of the UN as "lack[ing] regular access to enough safe and nutritious food for normal growth and development and an active and healthy life. (Food and Agriculture Organization of the United Nations, n.d.). Food insecurity ranges from mild to severe, from unreliable access to food, to reduced | 3 |
|---|---|---|
| | quality and variety of food, to reduced quantity of food (including skipping meals), to not eating for a day or more (Food and Agriculture Organization of the United Nations, n.d.). Food insecurity is more likely to affect women than men and is mostly likely to affect women and children of color. | |
| Food justice | A direct response to combatting food insecurity, particularly for those in marginalized communities. Individuals involved in the food justice movement seek to eliminate food insecurity by addressing food insecurity from a gendered, economic, racial, and political standpoint. | 3 |
| Heterosexism | Excluding or omitting the perspectives, experiences, cultures, and histories of gay and queer people and casting heterosexuality and heterosexual relationships as the norm. | 3 |
| Gender | Socially constructed and culturally specific roles, behaviors, and identities of being feminine, masculine, or a combination of traits. | 1 |

| Gender-expansive | An umbrella term for people whose gender expression and identity are beyond or outside a specific gender identity, category, or label. As an umbrella term, *gender-expansive* encompasses many different identities. Some gender-expansive people use this term when referencing their gender identity and some prefer other related terms. For example, | 1 |
|---|---|---|
| | • Some gender-expansive people identify with a spectrum of genders and may use the term *nonbinary*; <br> • some gender-expansive people identify primarily with a single gender and may use the term *transgender*; <br> • and still other gender-expansive people may identify without a gender and use the term *agender*. | |
| | As with all identity labels, it is important to honor the terms and language individuals identify with while also respecting that language can change over time. | |
| Global feminisms | The intentional study of feminisms from around the world. This study is grounded in an ethics of inclusion. Global feminisms explore local feminisms and justice movements, transnational approaches (or those that move beyond geographical boundaries), and global trends such as those in the UNs' Sustainable Development Goals. The Vanderbilt Global Feminisms Collaborative (n.d.) writes that | 1 |

| | | |
|---|---|---|
| | Global feminisms scholars are engaged in the study of boundaries associated with sex, gender, sexuality, class, race, ability, ethnicity, geography, identity, and membership—using both theoretical and empirical lenses. They are attentive to silence and marginalization, to citizenship politics (including migration, refugees, rights, and participation), to political economy (formal and informal), to society and culture, and to the environment (understood as the places where we live, work, play, and pray).<br><br>(para 3) | |
| Health disparities | According to the Centers for Disease Control and Prevention, "preventable differences in the burden of disease, injury, violence, or opportunities to achieve optimal health that are experienced by socially disadvantaged populations" (2020). Health disparities are most pronounced among historically and currently marginalized groups of people including communities of color, Indigenous communities, and members of the LGBTQIA+ community. | ?? |
| Intersectional environmentalism and intersectional environmental justice | A term was coined by Leah Thomas, an "eco-communicator, aka an environmentalist with a love for writing + creativity" (Thomas, n.d.). She defines intersectional environmentalism as | ?? |

| | an inclusive version of environmentalism that advocates for both the protection of people and the planet [and] acknowledges the overlap between systemic harm against Black, Indigenous, and people of color (BIPOC) communities and the Earth. The movement also recognizes the disproportional effects of climate change on other marginalized groups, including people with disabilities as well as women and gender minorities. (Capshaw-Mack, 2021)bx | |
|---|---|---|
| Intersectionality | A framework for understanding how multiple identities and *systems of oppressions* intersect to create specific experiences and conditions within systems. These experiences include systems of advantage (power and privilege) and disadvantage (discrimination and oppression). For example, these may include the compounding effects of racism and sexism; racism and heterosexism; or racism, sexism, and heterosexism. This framework centers the experiences and "voices of those experiencing overlapping, concurrent forms of oppression in order to understand outsider the depths of the inequalities and the relationships among them in any given context" (UN Women, 2020, para 5). Recognizing the first-person experiences and stories of individuals from historically marginalized and multiply marginalized backgrounds as important sites for knowledge is inherent to intersectional approaches. (See also descriptions of *Black feminisms* and *Kimberlé Crenshaw's* work, which we explore throughout this book.) | 3 |

| Interpersonal racism | The biases that occur between individuals related to their beliefs about race, ethnicity, and country of origin. These biases can be deep-seated, including beliefs about internalized oppression and internalized privilege, and they can present in overt and covert ways. | 6 |
|---|---|---|
| Intersex | A general term used for a variety of situations in which a person's reproductive anatomy doesn't fit the binary definitions of "female" or "male." | 1 |
| Liberal feminisms | A framework that operates *within* systems to improve them. Cornerstones of this framework include working toward equal opportunity, access, individual rights, liberty, and legislative equity (Fishman-Weaver, 2017). Establishing better sexual harassment or equal opportunity hiring practices are examples of initiatives that liberal feminists might advocate for. | 2 |
| Low-income countries (LICs) | The World Health Organization and the World Bank have moved away from referring to countries as "developing" or "developed" and now categorize countries by their gross domestic product (GDP) and gross national income. Using these statistics, countries can be classified as low income, middle income, or upper-middle income. Many of the LICs discussed in these lessons are located in the Global South. The income statistics are also imperfect, as some emerging economies have trouble estimating their GDP and as some more advanced economies have stark inequities within their countries. As with all the categorization, specificity matters. If you are researching a specific country, name that country. | 6 |

| Maternal health | The physical, emotional, and medical health of child-bearing people during pregnancy, childbirth, and the postnatal period. | 6 |
|---|---|---|
| Maternal mortality ratio (MMR) | According to the World Health Organization,<br><br>the number of maternal deaths during a given time period per 100,000 live births . . . It depicts the risk of maternal death relative to the number of live births and essentially captures the risk of death in a single pregnancy or a single live birth. (World Health Organization, n.d-a). | 6 |
| Margin | A concept to help us think about social space. The margins can be a philosophical or physical place (noun). Being in the margins is "to be part of the whole but outside the main body" (hooks, 2014b, p. xvii). This is where the verb *marginalize* comes from. | 3 |
| Patriarchy | A system of government, society, or family in which men hold power and women are systematically excluded from power. Feminist movements seek to dismantle patriarchal systems and establish more equitable systems. | 2 |
| Praxis | The intersection of action and theory. It is where you take what you learn and turn it into action. | 2 |

| Queer theory (and lesbian feminism) | A critical framework that challenges power dynamics related to gender and sexuality. Queer theory rejects essentialist (or pre-determined) definitions and binary thinking. Rather than assuming that categories of gender, sex, and sexuality are natural and fixed, queer theorists seek a more nuanced understanding of gender as dynamic and negotiated. This framework celebrates a full spectrum of identities. Queer theory frameworks are used in literary criticism, political criticism, sociology studies, and more layered accounts of history. (See especially Gloria Anzaldúa, Adrienne Rich, Judith Butler, and Eve Kosofsky Sedgwick.) | 2 |
|---|---|---|
| Radical feminisms | A framework that operates *beyond* systems to construct new structures and possibilities. Radical feminists believe that our systems are so deeply rooted in inequity and oppression they must be fundamentally deconstructed, reimagined, and built anew. A famous radical feminist text is Audre Lorde's essay "The Master's Tools Will Never Dismantle the Master's House" (2015). | 2 |
| Radical hope | The intentional practice of embracing possibility as a pathway forward. Radical hope asks us as participants to imagine that change is possible and to create space for new ideas and solutions, including those that represent a radical departure from the status quo (Fishman-Weaver & Walter, 2022). | 4 |
| Scholarship | The academic study of and/or commitment to learning at a high level. | 1 |

| Sex | A label (female or male) assigned at birth based on reproductive anatomy, chromosomes, and biology. | 1 |
|---|---|---|
| Social construct | An idea that has been created, accepted, and reinforced across a cultural group (e.g., gender and race) | 1 |
| Structural racism | The systematic advantages and disadvantages that are embedded in institutions. These structural systems systematically disadvantage communities of color through the cumulative impacts of cultural, political, historical forces. | 6 |
| Systems of oppression | The ways institutions, structures, and norms reinforce or perpetuate discrimination, including but not limited to sexism, racism, classism, heterosexism, ableism, and ageism. These systems can also be called the *matrix of domination*. Systems of oppression are socially and historically specific and connected to power. Patricia Hill Collins is a leading thought leader in this area. | 3 |
| Transgender | People whose gender does not align with the sex they were assigned at birth. For example, if a baby was assigned male at birth and later identifies as a girl/woman, she may be transgender (or trans). | 1 |
| Transnational feminisms | A methodology that seeks global action and understanding. It strives to move beyond individual nations or nation-states to engage in a more collective production of knowledge. | 1 |
| Underground Railroad | A cooperative system of abolitionists in the United States who worked to support enslaved peoples' escape to the North and Canada before 1863. | 5 |

| United Nations' Sustainable Development Goals (SDG) | The UNs' Sustainable Development plan outlines 17 goals called the SDGs for peace, prosperity, and wellbeing for humanity and the planet we share.<br><br>◆ SDG 1—No poverty<br>◆ SDG 2—Zero Hunger<br>◆ SDG 3—Good Health and Well-being<br>◆ SDG 4—Quality Education<br>◆ SDG 5—Gender Equality<br>◆ SDG 6—Clean Water and Sanitation<br>◆ SDG 7—Affordable and Clean Energy<br>◆ SDG 8—Decent Work and Economic Growth<br>◆ SDG 9—Industry, Innovation, and Infrastructure<br>◆ SDG 10—Reduced Inequalities<br>◆ SDG 11—Sustainable Cities and Communities<br>◆ SDG 12—Responsible Consumption and Production<br>◆ SDG 13—Climate Action<br>◆ SDG 14—Life Below Water<br>◆ SDG 15—Life on Land<br>◆ SDG 16—Peace, Justice, and Strong Institutions<br>◆ SDG 17—Partnerships for the Goals | 1 |
| Women's and Gender Studies (WGST) | An interdisciplinary study of the ways gender is constructed and how it affects our lived experiences and opportunities; a commitment to work toward greater justice and equity; and the intentional centering of stories, histories, and contributions of women, girls that are too often missing from curricula and media. | 1 |

# References

*1 in 3 people globally do not have access to safe drinking water—UNICEF, WHO.* (2019, June 18). World Health Organization. Retrieved January 13, 2022, from www.who.int/news/item/18-06-2019-1-in-3-people-globally-do-not-have-access-to-safe-drinking-water-unicef-who

*100 outstanding women nurse and midwife leaders.* (2020). YONM. Retrieved January 16, 2022, from https://yonm.org/?u=3baa3c42161aef075ad51675b&id=ba302cff37&e=3d213ca31

Abrams, S. (2018). *Minority leader: How to lead from the outside and make real change.* Henry Holt and Co.

Acosta, M., Ampaire, E., Okolo, W., & Twyman, J. (2015, June). *Gender and climate change in Uganda: Effects of policy and institutional frameworks.* Research Program on Climate Change, Agriculture and Food Security. Retrieved February 13, 2022, from www.wocan.org/sites/default/files/PACCA%20Gender%20Info%20Note%20Uganda.pdf

Adichie, C. N. (2009, October 7). The danger of a single story [Video]. *TED Talks.* www.ted.com/talks/chimamanda_ngozi_adichie_the_danger_of_a_single_story?language=en

Adichie, C. N. (2014). *We should all be feminists.* Vintage.

American Civil Liberties Union. (n.d.). *Tribute: The legacy of Ruth Bader Ginsburg and WRP staff.* Retrieved February 28, 2022, from www.aclu.org/other/tribute-legacy-ruth-baderginsburg-and-wrp-staff

American Psychological Association. (n.d.). *APA dictionary of psychology.* https://dictionary.apa.org/emotional-development

Amnesty International. (2021, October 11). *Its intersex awareness day—here are 5 myths we need to shatter.* www.amnesty.org/en/latest/news/2018/10/its-intersex-awareness-day-here-are-5-myths-we-need-to-shatter/

Angyal, C. (2018, March 28). Men write history, but women live it. *HuffPost.* Retrieved March 31, 2022, from www.huffpost.com/entry/opinion-angyal-womens-history-month_n_5a970857e4b0e6a52304517e

Archwy, A. (2021, April 12). *Krudas Cubensi wants the freedom of Cuba, of all countries, of all bodies.* Archyworldys. Retrieved January 3, 2022, from https://www.archyworldys.com/krudas-cubensi-wants-the-freedom-of-cuba-of-all-countries-of-all-bodies/

Armstead, R. (2007, Spring). "Growing the size of the Black woman": Feminist activism in Havana hip hop. *NWSA Journal, 19*(1), 106–117. www.jstor.org/stable/4317233

Artiga, S., Pham, O., Orgera, K., & Ranji, U. (2020, November 10). *Racial disparities in maternal and infant health: An overview—issue brief*. Kaiser Family Foundation. www.kff.org/report-section/racial-disparities-in-maternal-and-infant-health-an-overview-issue-brief/

The Art Story. (n.d.). *Feminist art movement overview*. Retrieved October 23, 2021, from www.theartstory.org/movement/feminist-art/

Artsy. (n.d.). *Christine Sun Kim—15 artworks, bio & shows on artsy*. Retrieved October 20, 2021, from www.artsy.net/artist/christine-sun-kim

Begnaud, D., & Reardon, S. (2021, December 16). Claudette Colvin, arrested for not giving up her seat for a White woman in 1955, has record expunged: "My name was cleared. I'm no longer a juvenile delinquent at 82." *CBS News*. https://www.cbsnews.com/news/claudette-colvin-record-expunged/

Belenky, M. F., Clinchy, B. M., Goldberger, N. R., & Tarule, J. M. (1997). *Women's ways of knowing (10th anniversary edition): The development of self, voice, and mind* (Revised ed.). Basic Books.

Bishop, K. (2001, March). This land knows me: Indigenous land rights. *Cultural Survival*. Retrieved January 12, 2022, from www.culturalsurvival.org/publications/cultural-survival-quarterly/land-knows-me-indigenous-land-rights

Bishop, R. S. (1990). Mirrors, windows, and sliding glass doors. *Perspectives*, 6(3), ix–xi.

Black mothers respond to our cover story on maternal mortality. (2018, April 19). *The New York Times Magazine*. Retrieved January 17, 2022, from www.nytimes.com/2018/04/19/magazine/black-mothers-respond-to-our-cover-story-on-maternal-mortality.html

Brooks, H. (2021, June 29). *Exploring a nonbinary approach to health*. NICHQ—National Institute for Children's Health Quality. www.nichq.org/insight/exploring-nonbinary-approach-health

Burke, T. (2020, July 17). *Get to know us founder*. Me Too Movement. https://metoomvmt.org/get-to-know-us/tarana-burke-founder/

Butler, J. (1999). *Gender trouble: Feminism and the subversion of identity* (2nd ed.). Routledge.

Capshaw-Mack, S. (2021, November 10). *A conversation with Leah Thomas, intersectional environmentalist*. State of the Planet. Retrieved February 13, 2022, from https://news.climate.columbia.edu/2021/11/10/a-conversation-with-leah-thomas-intersectional-environmentalist/

CBC Kids News. (2020, November 20). On national child day, meet clean water activist Autumn Peltier [Video]. *YouTube*. www.youtube.com/watch?v=A33XRMLBbOc

CBC News. (2018, March 22). Autumn Peltier, 13-year-old water advocate, addresses UN [Video]. *YouTube*. www.youtube.com/watch?v=zg60sr38oic

CDC. (2020). *Health disparities | DASH | CDC*. Center for Disease Control and Prevention. www.cdc.gov/healthyyouth/disparities/index.htm

Centers for Disease Control and Prevention. (2021, November 24). *Racism and health*. Retrieved December 21, 2021, from https://www.cdc.gov/healthequity/racism-disparities/index.html

Centers for Disease Control and Prevention. (2022, June 22). *Pregnancy mortality surveillance system*. Retrieved August 2, 2022, from www.cdc.gov/reproductivehealth/maternal-mortality/pregnancy-mortality-surveillance-system.htm?CDC_AA_refVal=https%3A%2F%2Fwww.cdc.gov%2Freproductivehealth%2Fmaternalinfanthealth%2Fpregnancy-mortality-surveillance-system.htm

Centers for Disease Control and Prevention. (n.d.). *Who are epidemiologists?* Retrieved January 18, 2022, from www.cdc.gov/careerpaths/k12teacher-roadmap/epidemiologists.html

Chewniski, M. (2010). Profile of Beverly Greene. In A. Rutherford (Ed.), *Psychology's feminist voices digital archive*. https://feministvoices.com/profiles/beverly-greene

Choi, C. (2020, October 21). Street art activism: What White people call vandalism. *Harvard Political Review*. https://harvardpolitics.com/street-art-activism/

Chuck, E., & Assefa, H. (2020, February 9). She hoped to shine a light on maternal mortality among Native Americans. Instead, she became a statistic of it. *NBC News*. Retrieved January 18, 2022, from www.nbcnews.com/news/us-news/she-hoped-shine-light-maternal-mortality-among-native-americans-instead-n1131951

CNN—bell hooks. (2000, February 17). *CNN*. Retrieved March 20, 2022, from http://edition.cnn.com/chat/transcripts/2000/2/hooks/index.html

Collins, P. H. (1986). Learning from the outsider within: The sociological significance of Black feminist thought. *Social Problems*, 33(6), S14–S32. https://doi.org/10.2307/800672

Collins, P. H. (2008). *Black feminist thought: Knowledge, consciousness, and the politics of empowerment (Routledge Classics)* (1st ed.). Routledge.

Combahee River Collective. (2015). A Black feminist statement. In C. Moraga & G. Anzaldúa (Eds.), *This bridge called my back: Writings by radical women of color* (4th ed., pp. 210–218). State University of New York Press.

Compton, J. (2018, February 22). For gay parents, first comes the baby—then comes the debt. *NBC News*. Retrieved April 7, 2022, from www.nbcnews.com/feature/nbc-out/gay-couples-having-kids-it-s-not-easy-or-hard-n850086

*Convention on the elimination of all forms of discrimination against women*. (n.d.). UN Women. Retrieved January 9, 2022, from www.un.org/womenwatch/daw/cedaw/

Crenshaw, K. (1989). Demarginalizing the intersection of race and sex: A Black feminist critique of antidiscrimination doctrine, feminist theory and anti-racist policies. *University of Chicago Legal Forum, 140*(1), 139–167.

Dalidayblue. (2021, November 10). Navigating life with a newborn in our highly homophobic culture is hard at times. Internalized homophobia is difficult to challenge [Instagram]. *Instagram.* www.instagram.com/p/CWHb78jpN4jFfNe-20yS4KX3d8-1y82lCDJikg0/

Daly, J. (2012, December 20). The evocative world of the six-word memoir: A Q&A with new TED ebook author Larry Smith. *TED Blog.* https://blog.ted.com/the-evocative-world-of-the-six-word-memoir-a-qa-with-new-ted-ebook-author-larry-smith/

D'Ambrosio, A. (2022, February 10). Here's how ob/gyns can create gender-affirming environments. *MedPage Today.* www.medpagetoday.com/special-reports/exclusives/97128

Darwin, Z., & Greenfield, M. (2019). Mothers and others: The invisibility of LGBTQ people in reproductive and infant psychology. *Journal of Reproductive and Infant Psychology, 37*(4), 341–343. https://doi.org/10.1080/02646838.2019.1649919

Diaz, N. (2014, March 29). Body as land. Body is land. *The Best American Poetry.* Retrieved December 13, 2021, from https://blog.bestamericanpoetry.com/the_best_american_poetry/2014/03/body-as-land-body-is-land.html

Douglas, T. M. O. (2013). Confessions of a border crossing *brotha*-scholar: Teaching race with all of me. In D. J. Davis & P. Boyer (Eds.), *Social justice and racism in the college classroom: Perspectives from different voices* (pp. 57–72). Emerald Publishing Group Ltd.

Earthday.org. (2019, June 6). School strike for climate: A day in the life of Ugandan student striker Leah Namugerwa. *Earth Day.* Retrieved February 12, 2022, from www.earthday.org/school-strike-for-climate-a-day-in-the-life-of-fridays-for-future-uganda-student-striker-leah-namugerwa/

Enos, T. (2018, September 13). 8 Things you should know about two spirit people. *Indian Country Today.* https://indiancountrytoday.com/archive/8-misconceptions-things-know-two-spirit-people

Everett, B. G., Kominiarek, M. A., Mollborn, S., Adkins, D. E., & Hughes, T. L. (2018). Sexual orientation disparities in pregnancy and infant outcomes. *Maternal and Child Health Journal, 23*(1), 72–81. https://doi.org/10.1007/s10995-018-2595-x

*FAQ: Harriet Tubman.* (n.d.). Harriet Tubman Historical Society. Retrieved January 19, 2022, from www.harriet-tubman.org/facts-kids/

*Feminism 101.* (2007b, August 27). Red Letter Press. Retrieved September 6, 2022, from http://www.redletterpress.org/feminism101.html

Fishman-Weaver, K. (2017). A call to praxis: Using gendered organizational theory to center radical hope in schools. *Journal of Organizational Theory in Education, 2*(1), 1–14.

Fishman-Weaver, K. (2018). *Wholehearted teaching of gifted young women*. Prufrock Press.

Fishman-Weaver, K., & Walter, S. (2022). *Connected classrooms: A person-centered approach to online, blended, and in-person learning*. Solution Tree.

Food and Agriculture Organization of the United Nations. (n.d.). *Hunger and food insecurity*. Retrieved February 12, 2022, from www.fao.org/hunger/en/

Free & Equal United Nations for LGBTI Equality. (n.d.). *Violence against lesbian, gay, bisexual or transgender people*. https://www.unfe.org/wp-content/uploads/2018/10/Violence-English.pdf

Gallant, D. (2020, September 24). *Autumn Peltier*. The Canadian Encyclopedia. Retrieved January 12, 2022, from www.thecanadianencyclopedia.ca/en/article/autumn-peltier

Garrison Institute. (2016, November 1). *Recovering our reciprocal relationship with the land*. Retrieved January 13, 2022, from www.garrisoninstitute.org/blog/recovering-reciprocal-relationship-land/

Gay, G. (2002). Preparing for culturally responsive teaching. *Journal of Teacher Education, 53*(2), 106–116.

Gettleman, J. (2018, February 17). The peculiar position of India's third gender. *The New York Times*. www.nytimes.com/2018/02/17/style/india-third-gender-hijras-transgender.html

Giovanni, N. (2010). *Quilting the Black-eyed pea: Poems and not quite poems* (Reprint ed.). William Morrow.

Global Feminisms Collaborative. (n.d.). *Global feminisms collaborative—GFC home*. Vanderbilt College of Arts and Science. https://as.vanderbilt.edu/archived/gfc/www.vanderbilt.edu/gfc/

Global News. (2018, March 22). World water day: Indigenous Canadian teen addresses UN general assembly [Video]. *YouTube*. www.youtube.com/watch?v=A6LcaTWTx8g

Gorman, A. (2021). *Call us what we carry*. Van Haren Publishing.

Green, C. (2018, May 10). *7 facts about maternal health you should know*. United Nations Foundation. Retrieved January 15, 2022, from https://unfoundation.org/blog/post/7-facts-about-maternal-health-you-should-know/

Green, E. L. (2019, November 6). Flint's children suffer in class after years of drinking the lead-poisoned water. *The New York Times*. Retrieved April 12, 2022, from www.nytimes.com/2019/11/06/us/politics/flint-michigan-schools.html?

Greene, B. A. (1986). When the therapist is White and the patient is Black: Considerations for psychotherapy in the feminist heterosexual and lesbian communities. *Women & Therapy*, 5(2–3), 41–65. https://doi.org/10.1300/J015V05N02_05

*Harriet Tubman*. (2009, October 29). History. Retrieved January 19, 2022, from www.history.com/topics/black-history/harriet-tubman

*Harriet Tubman*. (2018, February 28). Biography. Retrieved January 19, 2022, from www.biography.com/activist/harriet-tubman

Headlee, C. (Host). (2019, October 22). Harriet's legacy today: Strength, courage, & triumph (No. 4) [Audio podcast episode]. In *Following Harriet*. Virginia Tourism Corporation. https://podcasts.apple.com/us/podcast/harriets-legacy-today-strength-courage-triumph/id1483073168?i=1000454411864

Henry, R. (2015, March 24). The roots of the word "feminism". *KMUW—NPR*. Retrieved December 27, 2021, from www.kmuw.org/past-and-present/2015-03-24/the-roots-of-the-word-feminism

*History of international women's day*. (n.d.). International Women's Day. Retrieved January 9, 2022, from www.internationalwomensday.com/Activity/15586/The-history-of-IWD

Holcomb, B. (2021). *Ladyboys (Kathoeys) | Encyclopedia.com*. Encyclopedia.Com. www.encyclopedia.com/social-sciences/encyclopedias-almanacs-transcripts-and-maps/ladyboys-kathoeys

hooks, b. (1989). Choosing the margin as a space of radical openness. *Framework: The Journal of Cinema and Media*, 36, 15–23. www.jstor.org/stable/44111660

hooks, b. (2002). *Communion: The female search for love (Love song to the Nation, 2)*. William Morrow Paperbacks.

hooks, b. (2014a). *Ain't I a woman: Black women and feminism* (2nd ed.). Routledge.

hooks, b. (2014b). *Feminist theory: From margin to center* (3rd ed.). Routledge.

hooks, b. (2020). *Feminism is for everybody: Passionate politics*. South End Press.

Horton, C. (2021, May 26). What do you mean by abolition? *Anthropology News*. www.anthropology-news.org/articles/what-do-you-mean-by-abolition/

HRC Staff. (2020, November 23). Two spirit and LGBTQ+ identities: Today and centuries ago. *HRC*. www.hrc.org/news/two-spirit-and-lgbtq-idenitites-today-and-centuries-ago

Hughes, B. (2017, February 28). Why were women written out of history? An interview with Bettany Hughes. *English Heritage Blog*. Retrieved January 9, 2022, from https://blog.english-heritage.org.uk/women-written-history-interview-bettany-hughes/

Hunt, M. E. (2016, March 4). Sally ride and the quest for social space. *Feminist Studies in Religion*. www.fsrinc.org/sally-ride-social-space/

Ibrahim, S. (2021, December 21). Stanford community reflects on passing of Black feminist scholar bell hooks '73. *The Stanford Daily*. https://stanforddaily.com/2021/12/22/stanford-community-reflects-on-passing-of-black-feminist-scholar-bell-hooks-73/

Igbo women campaign for rights (The Women's War) in Nigeria, 1929. (n.d.). *Global Nonviolent Action Database*. Retrieved January 9, 2022, from https://nvdatabase.swarthmore.edu/content/igbo-women-campaign-rights-womens-war-nigeria-1929

Illich, L., & Alter Smith, M. (2018, January). Teach living poets. *Teach Living Poets*. https://teachlivingpoets.com

Indian Health Service. (n.d.). *Two-spirit | health resources*. Indian Health Service The Federal.

Irving, S. [@shalonirvingphd]. (n.d.). *Tweets* [Twitter Profile]. Retrieved January 18, 2022, from https://twitter.com/shalonirvingphd

Isaacs-Thomas, I. (2021, May 26). For many pregnant trans people, competent medical care is hard to find. *PBS NewsHour*. www.pbs.org/newshour/health/for-many-pregnant-trans-people-competent-medical-care-is-hard-to-find

Jacques, K. (2019, November 12). Jamie Margolin's climate action movement gathers momentum. *USGBC*. Retrieved February 13, 2022, from www.usgbc.org/articles/jamie-margolin-s-climate-action-movement-gathers-momentum

James, J. (2022, January 27). Jackson water crisis again impacts schools. *Mississippi Today*. Retrieved April 12, 2022, from https://mississippitoday.org/2022/01/27/jackson-water-crisis-again-impacts-schools/

Johari, A. (2014, April 17). Hijra, Kothi, Aravani: A quick guide to transgender terminology. *Scroll.In*. Retrieved March 23, 2022, from https://scroll.in/article/662023/hijra-kothi-aravani-a-quick-guide-to-transgender-terminology

Johnson, A. E., & Wilkinson, K. K. (2021). *All we can save: Truth, courage, and solutions for the climate crisis*. One World.

Kelly, S. (2020, August 11). The future is intersectional. *Climable.Org*. Retrieved February 13, 2022, from https://climable.org/blog/2020/8/5/intersectional-future

Kendall, M. (2020). *Hood feminism: Notes from the women that a movement forgot*. Penguin.

The Kennedy Center. (n.d.). Las Krudas. *The Kennedy Center: Las Krudas*. Retrieved February 23, 2022, from www.kennedy-center.org/artists/l/la-ln/-las-krudas/

Kimmerer, R. (2013). *Braiding sweetgrass: Indigenous wisdom, scientific knowledge, and the teachings of plants*. Milkweed Editions.

Kozhimannil, K. B. (2020). Indigenous maternal health—A crisis demanding attention. *JAMA Health Forum, 1*(5), e200517. http://doi.org/10.1001/jamahealthforum.2020.0517

Kozleski, E. B. (2010). Culturally responsive teaching matters! *The Equity Alliance at ASU.* www.un.org/sustainabledevelopment/gender-equality/

Krudas Cubensi. (n.d.). *Krudas Cubensi.* Retrieved February 23, 2022, from https://krudascubensi.com/bio-press-krudas-cubensi/

Kwan, R. O. (2021, December 6). R.O. Kwon on our climate in crisis. *Greenpeace USA.* https://www.greenpeace.org/usa/stories/ro-kwon-on-our-climate-in-crisis/#:%7E:text=I%20want%20to%20live%20on,and%20then%20act%20as%20if%3F

Laughlin, K. A., Gallagher, J., Cobble, D. S., Boris, E., Nadasen, P., Gilmore, S., & Zarnow, L. (2010). Is it time to jump ship? Historians rethink the waves metaphor. *Feminist Formations,* 76–135.

Lawless, J. (2022, March 22). Greta Thunberg aims to drive change with 'the climate book'. *AP News.* Retrieved April 5, 2022, from https://apnews.com/article/climate-entertainment-environment-environment-greta-thunberg-80a06f634e938089b8a87edc20d0c7ba

Leah Namugerwa. (n.d.). *Responses to Greta Thunberg in international media.* Retrieved February 13, 2022, from https://pages.stolaf.edu/responses-to-thunberg/for-students/global-youth-activists/leah-namugerwa/

Levine, S., & Rao, A. (2020, October 7). In 2013 the supreme court gutted voting rights—how has it changed the US? *The Guardian.* Retrieved April 5, 2022, from www.theguardian.com/us-news/2020/jun/25/shelby-county-anniversary-voting-rights-act-consequences

Lopez, G. R., Gonzalez, M. L., & Fierro, E. (2006). Educational leadership along the US-Mexico border: Crossing borders/embracing hybridity/building bridges. In *Leadership for social justice: Making revolutions in education* (pp. 279–306). Pearson.

Lorde, A. (2015). The Master's tools will never dismantle the Master's house. In C. Moraga & G. Anzaldúa's (Eds.), *This bridge called my back: Writings by radical women of color* (pp. 94–103). Suny Press.

Love, B. (2020). *We want to do more than survive: Abolitionist teaching and the pursuit of educational freedom* (Illustrated ed.). Beacon Press.

Mancino, J. (2019, May 24). Meet the Kathoey: An intro to Thailand's unique transgender culture. *Jetset Times.* https://jetsettimes.com/lgbtq/meet-the-kathoey/

Marinaro, C. (2021, March 22). Nwanyeruwa—The women's revolt against British colonialism. *The Heroine Collective.* Retrieved April 12, 2022, from www.theheroinecollective.com/nwanyeruwa-the-womens-revolt-against-british-colonialism/

Martin, N., & Montagne, R. (2017a, May 12). U.S. has the worst rate of maternal deaths in the developed world. *NPR*. Retrieved January 16, 2022, from www.npr.org/2017/05/12/528098789/u-s-has-the-worst-rate-of-maternal-deaths-in-the-developed-world

Martin, N., & Montagne, R. (2017b, December 7). Black mothers keep dying after giving birth. Shalon Irving's story explains why. *NPR*. Retrieved January 16, 2022, from www.npr.org/2017/12/07/568948782/black-mothers-keep-dying-after-giving-birth-shalon-irvings-story-explains-why

Martin, N., & Montagne, R. (2017c, December 7). Nothing protects Black women from dying in pregnancy and childbirth. *ProPublica*. Retrieved January 16, 2022, from www.propublica.org/article/nothing-protects-black-women-from-dying-in-pregnancy-and-childbirth

Martinez, C., & Carrington, K. (2021). Re-thinking gender, artivism and choices. Cultures of equality emerging from urban peripheries. *Frontiers in Sociology*, 6. https://doi.org/10.3389/fsoc.2021.637564

*Maternal health*. (n.d.). United Nations Population Fund. Retrieved January 15, 2022, from www.unfpa.org/maternal-health

*Maternal mortality*. (2019, September 19). World Health Organization. Retrieved January 15, 2022, from www.who.int/news-room/fact-sheets/detail/maternal-mortalitycy-and-childbirth

Mayo Clinic. (2021, October 16). *Miscarriage—Symptoms and causes*. www.mayoclinic.org/diseases-conditions/pregnancy-loss-miscarriage/symptoms-causes/syc-20354298

*Meet Nobel Peace laureate Rigoberta Menchú Tum*. (2017, July 17). Nobel Women's Initiative. Retrieved January 9, 2022, from https://nobelwomensinitiative.org/laureate/rigoberta-menchu-tum/0/

Michels, D. (2015). *Sojourner truth*. National Women's History Museum. Retrieved November 10, 2021, from www.womenshistory.org/education-resources/biographies/sojourner-truth

Miranda, D. *Prayer of prayers*. Retrieved January 23, 2022, from https://orion-magazine.org/article/women-standing-rock/

Modi, M. N., Palmer, S., & Armstrong, A. (2014). The role of violence against women act in addressing intimate partner violence: A public health issue. *Journal of Women's Health*, 23(3), 253–259. https://doi.org/10.1089/jwh.2013.4387

Morris, M. (2018). *Pushout: The criminalization of Black girls in schools* (First Trade Paper ed.). The New Press.

Nadkarni, A., & Subhalakshmi, G. (2017). Transnational feminism. *Oxford Bibliographies Online in Literary and Critical Theory*. http://doi.org/10.1093/obo/9780190221911-0006.https://www.oxfordbibliographies.com/view/document/obo-9780190221911/obo-9780190221911-0006.xml?rskey=kqd26P&result=1&q=Transnational++feminism#firstMatch

Nassar, D., & Gjesdal, K. (2022, March 8). International women's day: Feminist philosophy with Clara Zetkin. *OUPblog*. Retrieved April 1, 2022, from https://blog.oup.com/2022/03/international-womens-day-feminist-philosophy-with-clara-zetkin/

National Abolition Hall of Fame and Museum. (n.d.). *Sojourner truth*. Retrieved November 14, 2021, from www.nationalabolitionhalloffameandmuseum.org/sojourner-truth.html

National Organization for Women. (n.d.). *Equal rights amendment—National Organization for Women*. https://now.org/resource/equal-rights-ammendment/

The National Women's Hall of Fame. (n.d.). *Parks, Rosa. National women's hall of fame*. Retrieved February 28, 2022, from www.womenofthehall.org/inductee/rosa-parks/

NBC News. (2020, February 7). Pregnant mom died while bringing attention to native American maternal mortality [Video]. *YouTube*. www.youtube.com/watch?v=jOYeqQoJF1I

Nepal sees huge rise in maternal deaths as Covid keeps women at home. (2021). *The Guardian*. Retrieved January 16, 2022, from www.theguardian.com/global-development/2021/jul/15/nepal-sees-huge-rise-in-maternal-deaths-as-covid-keeps-women-at-home

Nineteenth amendment to the United States constitution. (n.d.). *Wikipedia*. Retrieved January 20, 2022, from https://en.wikipedia.org/wiki/Nineteenth_Amendment_to_the_United_States_Constitution

Nove, A., Friberg, I. K., de Bernis, L., McConville, F., Moran, A. C., Najjemba, M., ten Hoope-Bender, P., Tracy, S., & Homer, C. S. E. (2021). Potential impact of midwives in preventing and reducing maternal and neonatal mortality and stillbirths: A Lives Saved Tool modelling study. *The Lancet Global Health*, *9*(1), e24–e32. https://doi.org/10.1016/s2214-109x(20)30397-1

Oxfam. (2019). *Gender inequalities and food insecurity: Ten years after the food price crisis, why are women farmers still food-insecure?* www.oxfamnovib.nl/Files/rapporten/2019/20190715%20bp-gender-inequalities-food-insecurity-150719-en.pdf

Pattanaik, D. (2019, April 20). The Hijra legacy. *Devdutt*. Retrieved March 23, 2022, from https://devdutt.com/articles/the-hijra-legacy/

Poetry Foundation. (n.d.). *Nikki Giovanni*. Retrieved January 4, 2022, from www.poetryfoundation.org/poets/nikki-giovanni

Pruitt, S. (2021, March 8). How the Mirabal sisters helped topple a dictator. *History*. Retrieved January 9, 2022, from www.history.com/news/mirabal-sisters-trujillo-dictator

*Research guides: The Dakota Access Pipeline: Native American perspectives: Home.* (2020, July 7). UNM University Libraries. Retrieved January 15, 2022, from https://libguides.unm.edu/DAPL

Rich, A. (2003). *What is found there: Notebooks on poetry and politics* (Expanded ed.). W. W. Norton & Company.

Rise Art. (2021, January 7). *A guide to the feminist art movement's history & contemporary impact.* www.riseart.com/guide/2418/guide-to-the-feminist-art-movement

*Role in the Civil War: Harriet Tubman.* (n.d.). Harriet Tubman Historical Society. Retrieved January 19, 2022, from www.harriet-tubman.org/role-in-the-civil-war/

*Rosa Parks.* (2018, February 27). Biography. Retrieved January 20, 2022, from www.biography.com/activist/rosa-parks

Roy, A. (2004). *An ordinary person's guide to empire* (1st ed.). South End Press.

*Rukumani (Ruku) Tripathi.* (2020, June 17). Women Deliver. Retrieved January 16, 2022, from https://womendeliver.org/classmember/rukumani-ruku-tripathi/

School Nutrition Association. (n.d.). *School meal trends & stats.* Retrieved February 15, 2022, from https://schoolnutrition.org/aboutschoolmeals/schoolmealtrendsstats/

*SDG 6: Ensure availability and sustainable management of water and sanitation for all.* (n.d.). UN Women. Retrieved January 13, 2022, from www.unwomen.org/en/news/in-focus/women-and-the-sdgs/sdg-6-clean-water-sanitation

*Shamsia Hassani—Official website.* (2021). Shamsia Hassani. www.shamsiahassani.net/

Shiva, V. (2009). Women and the gendered politics of food. *Philosophical Topics*, *37*(2), 17–32. https://doi.org/10.5840/philtopics20093722

Simmons, D. (2012, August 29). Guest blog: Emancipatory education: Dena Simmons on teaching for social justice in middle school. *Feminist Teacher*. Retrieved December 10, 2021, from https://feministteacher.com/2012/08/29/guest-blog-emancipatory-education-dena-simmons-on-teaching-for-social-justice-in-middle-school/#more-1144

Sitaula, S., Basnet, T., Agrawal, A., Manandhar, T., Das, D., & Shretha, P. (2021, July 1). Prevalence and risk factors for maternal mortality at a tertiary care centre in Eastern Nepal-retrospective cross sectional study—BMC Pregnancy and Childbirth. *BioMed Central*. Retrieved January 16, 2022, from https://bmcpregnancychildbirth.biomedcentral.com/articles/10.1186/s12884-021-03920-4

Stein, P. (2017, January 31). The woman who started the Women's March with a Facebook post reflects: 'It was mind-boggling'. *Washington Post*.

Retrieved January 20, 2022, from www.washingtonpost.com/news/local/wp/2017/01/31/the-woman-who-started-the-womens-march-with-a-facebook-post-reflects-it-was-mind-boggling/

Superville, D. R. (2017, March 8). Few women run the nation's school districts. Why? *Education Week*. www.edweek.org/leadership/few-women-run-the-nations-school-districts-why/2016/11

Taylor, K. (2020, July 20). Until Black women are free, none of us will be free. *The New Yorker*. www.newyorker.com/news/our-columnists/until-black-women-are-free-none-of-us-will-be-free

Thomas, L. (n.d.). About: Green Girl Leah. *Green Girl Leah*. Retrieved February 13, 2022, from www.greengirlleah.com/about-2

Thulin, L. (2020, January 15). Why the equal rights amendment is still not part of the constitution. *Smithsonian Magazine*. Retrieved January 20, 2022, from www.smithsonianmag.com/history/equal-rights-amendment-96-years-old-and-still-not-part-constitution-heres-why-180973548/

*Timeline: Women of the world, unite!* (n.d.). UN Women. Retrieved January 9, 2022, from https://interactive.unwomen.org/multimedia/timeline/womenunite/en/index.html#/1840

The Trevor Project. (n.d.). *The Trevor Project national survey*. Retrieved February 20, 2022, from www.thetrevorproject.org/survey-2021/?section=Introduction

Truth, S. (1851). *Ain't I a woman?* Learning for Justice. www.learningforjustice.org/classroom-resources/texts/aint-i-a-woman

Tuck, E. (2009). Suspending damage: A letter to communities. *Harvard Educational Review, 79*, 409–428.

Tucker, J., & Ewing-Nelson, C. (2020, October). Black, non-Hispanic women and Latinas are facing severe COVID-19 impact. *Women's National Law Center*. Retrieved February 10, 2022, from https://nwlc.org/wp-content/uploads/2020/10/pulseFS-1.pdf

UNA-UK. (2021, October 22). *It's not too late*. Retrieved April 4, 2022, from https://una.org.uk/magazine/2021-1/its-not-too-late

UN Climate Change. (2018, December 10). Greta Thunberg at COP24: "You are never too small to make difference" [Video]. *YouTube*. www.youtube.com/watch?v=CAJuX7xed8o

UNFPA. (2021, October 5). Eager to get into action to improve maternal health, Nepal midwives await govt's recruitment plan. *UNFPA Nepal*. Retrieved January 16, 2022, from https://nepal.unfpa.org/en/news/eager-get-action-improve-maternal-health-nepal-midwives-await-govts-recruitment-plan

UNICEF. (n.d.). *Girls' education*. https://www.unicef.org/education/girls-education

United Nations. (2014, September 22). Emma Watson at the HeForShe campaign 2014—official UN video [Video]. *YouTube*. www.youtube.com/watch?v=gkjW9PZBRfk

United Nations. (2020). United Nations: Gender equality and women's empowerment. *United Nations Sustainable Development*. Retrieved September 3, 2021, from www.un.org/sustainabledevelopment/gender-equality/

United Nations. (n.d.-a). Goal 3: Ensure healthy lives and promote well-being for all at all ages. *United Nations Sustainable Development*. Retrieved January 15, 2022, from www.un.org/sustainabledevelopment/health/

United Nations. (n.d.-b). *United Nations: Goal 5: Achieve Gender Equality and Empower All Women and Girls*. https://www.un.org/sustainabledevelopment/gender-equality/

United Nations. (n.d.-c). Goal 5: Gender equality—SDG tracker. *Our World in Data*. Retrieved September 3, 2021, from https://sdg-tracker.org/gender-equality

United Nations. (n.d.-d). *What Is Climate Change?* https://www.un.org/en/climatechange/what-is-climate-change

United Nations. (n.d.-e). *Women's job market participation stagnating at less than 50% for the past 25 years, finds UN report*. https://www.un.org/en/desa/women%E2%80%99s-job-market-participation-stagnating-less-50-past-25-years-finds-un-report

United Nations Department of Economic and Social Affairs. (2017). *World day of social justice 2017 | DISD*. www.un.org/development/desa/dspd/international-days/world-day-of-social-justice/world-day-of-social-justice-2017.html

United Nations Population Fund. (2018, March). *Indigenous women's maternal health and maternal mortality*. www.unfpa.org/resources/indigenous-womens-maternal-health-and-maternal-mortality

United Nations Statistics Division. (n.d.). *Goal 2: End hunger, achieve food security and improved nutrition and promote sustainable agriculture—SDG indicators*. United Nations. Retrieved March 16, 2022, from https://unstats.un.org/sdgs/report/2016/goal-02/

UN Women. (2020, July 1). *Intersectional feminism: what it means and why it matters right now*. www.unwomen.org/en/news/stories/2020/6/explainer-intersectional-feminism-what-it-means-and-why-it-matters

UN Women. (2021-a, January 15). Facts and figures: Women's leadership and political participation. *UN Women*. https://www.unwomen.org/en/what-we-do/leadership-and-political-participation/facts-and-figures

UN Women. (2021-b, March 5). Four facts you need to know about gender and poverty today. *UN Women*. https://data.unwomen.org/features/four-facts-you-need-know-about-gender-and-poverty-today

UN Women. (2022, February). Facts and figures: Ending violence against women. *UN Women*. https://www.unwomen.org/en/what-we-do/ending-violence-against-women/facts-and-figures

UN Women. (n.d.). Equal pay for work of equal value. *UN Women*. https://www.unwomen.org/en/news/in-focus/csw61/equal-pay

Villarosa, L. (2018, April 15). Why America's Black mothers and babies are in a life-or-death crisis. *The New York Times*. Retrieved January 17, 2022, from www.nytimes.com/2018/04/11/magazine/black-mothers-babies-death-maternal-mortality.html

*Violence against women act*. (n.d.). Futures without Violence. Retrieved January 23, 2022, from www.futureswithoutviolence.org/policy-advocacy-2/violence-against-women-act/

Walker, A. (1983). *In search of our mothers' gardens: Womanist prose* (1st ed.). Harcourt Brace Jovanovich.

*Where are the women: A report on the status of women in the United States social studies standards*. (2017). National Women's History Museum. www.womenshistory.org/sites/default/files/museum-assets/document/2018-01/NWHM_Status-of-Women-in-State-Social-Studies-Standards.pdf

The White House. (2021, April 14). *A proclamation on Black maternal health week, 2021*. Retrieved April 3, 2022, from www.whitehouse.gov/briefing-room/presidential-actions/2021/04/13/a-proclamation-on-black-maternal-health-week-2021/

Wise, A. (2022, February 9). *Senators announce a deal to reauthorize the Violence Against Women Act*. NPR. https://choice.npr.org/index.html?origin=www.npr.org/2022/02/09/1079717258/senators-announce-a-deal-to-reauthorize-the-violence-against-women-act

*Women's march*. (2018, January 5). History. Retrieved January 20, 2022, from www.history.com/this-day-in-history/womens-march

*Working together to reduce Black maternal mortality*. (n.d.). Centers for Disease Control and Prevention. Retrieved January 15, 2022, from www.cdc.gov/healthequity/features/maternal-mortality/index.html

The World. (2020, February 13). Artist Christine Sun Kim on 'deaf rage,' the Super Bowl and the power. The World from PRX.

The World Bank. (n.d.). *Food security and COVID-19*. World Bank. Retrieved February 16, 2022, from www.worldbank.org/en/topic/agriculture/brief/food-security-and-covid-19#:%7E:text=Using%20a%20different%20indicator%20that,million%20in%20just%20one%20year

World Food Program USA. (n.d.-a). *COVID-19 pandemic is causing global hunger in poor countries*. Retrieved February 10, 2022, from www.wfpusa.org/drivers-of-hunger/covid-19/

World Food Program USA. (n.d.-b). *Gender inequality is causing more women to suffer from hunger*. Retrieved February 10, 2022, from www.wfpusa.org/drivers-of-hunger/gender-inequality/

World Health Organization. (n.d.-a). *Indicator metadata registry details*. The Global Health Observatory. Retrieved December 30, 2021, from www.who.int/data/gho/indicator-metadata-registry/imr-details/26#:%7E:text=Limitations%3A,accurate%20assessment%20of%20maternal%20mortality

World Health Organization. (n.d.-b). *Maternal health*. World Health Organization Regional Office for Africa. Retrieved January 15, 2022, from www.afro.who.int/health-topics/maternal-health

*Zero Hour*. (n.d.). Zero Hour. Retrieved February 13, 2022, from http://thisiszerohour.org/

*Zero Hour: Our actions*. (n.d.). Zero Hour. Retrieved February 13, 2022, from http://thisiszerohour.org/our-actions/

Zoeller, C. (2021, October 25). *Climate hero: Xiye Bastida*. One Earth. Retrieved February 13, 2022, from www.oneearth.org/climate-hero-xiye-bastida/

# Index

19th Amendment 125–126

abolition 44–55, 116–117; *see also* Truth, Sojourner; Tubman, Harriet
Abrams, Stacy 158–160
Adichie, Chimamanda 47–48, 59, 88–90, 103
advocacy 30, 44–50, 115; feminism 47; legal action and 45–46; gender 49–50, 54; *see also* upstander
allyship 44–46, 177; *and* performative allyship 87
artivism 165–166, 169; *see also* Hassani, Shamsia; Kim, Christine ("CK") Sun; Las Krudas
asset-based approaches 22

Bastida, Xiye 84; *see also* climate justice
binary 35, 38–39, 44; *see also* queer theory
Black feminisms 22, 44, 52, 70, 78; *see also* Collins, Patricia Hill; The Combahee River Collective; hooks, bell; intersectionality; Truth, Sojourner

cisgender 36, 153; *see also* gender-expansive; transgender
Clifton, Adrian 60–61
climate justice 80–84
Clingan, Jill viiii, 6–7
Collins, Patricia Hill 72, 76–79; *see also* intersectionality; systems of oppression
colonization 34, 39–40, 133

Colvin, Claudette 111–112, 127; *see also* Parks, Rosa; racial justice
The Combahee River Collective 77–79
Crenshaw, Kimberlé 52, 62, 65–66; *see also* Black feminisms; intersectionality
critical consciousness 53–54; *see also* hooks, bell

DeCastro, Lisa 174–175
disaggregated data 148
Domingues, Stefani 162–164

Equal Rights Amendment 126, 160
equality 32–33
equity 32–33
Eurocentrism 98

feminism 21, 29, 31, 33, 51, 120; *see also* Black feminisms; global feminisms; hooks, bell; liberal feminisms; queer theory; radical feminisms; transnational feminisms
Feminist Art Movement 166
Fishman-Weaver, Kathryn viiii, 5–6
food insecurity 91–92, 94–97; *see also* food justice; United Nations Sustainable Development Goals (SDG)
food justice 91, 97; *see also* food insecurity; United Nations Sustainable Development Goals (SDG)

gender-expansive 34, 36; *see also* hijra;
    kathoey; transgender; two spirit
gender justice 120–124; *see also*
    Collins, Patricia Hill; Las Krudas;
    Truth, Sojourner
Giovanni, Nikki 76, 158
Glick, Elisa 9–11
global feminisms 25–26, 93
Gorman, Amanda 67, 114
Greene, Beverly 98

Hassani, Shamsia 169, 173; *see also*
    artivism
heterosexism 98
hijra 34, 37, 40–41; *see also* transgender
Hirsi, Isra 83–84; *see also* climate
    justice
hooks, bell 42, 46, 51–54; *see also*
    Black feminisms; Truth, Sojourner

imposter syndrome 57–58
intersectional environmentalism
    80; intersectional environmental
    justice 80
intersectionality 22, 76; *see also* Collins,
    Patricia Hill; Crenshaw, Kimberlé
intersex 35–36
Irving, Shalon 159–160; *see also*
    maternal health

justice 42; *see also* climate justice;
    gender justice; racial justice

kathoey 34, 37, 40; *see also* transgender
Kendall, Mikki 74, 92–94; *see also*
    food insecurity; food justice
Kim, Christine ("CK") Sun 170–173;
    *see also* artivism

Lane-Bonds, Dena 105–106
Las Krudas 170; *see also* artivism

liberal feminisms 32–33, 52
low-income countries (LICs) 138

mandated reporting 23–24
Margolin, Jamie 82–83; *see also*
    climate justice
maternal health 110, 136, 138–139,
    149, 153; Black women and
    149–151; the COVID pandemic
    and 146–147; Indigenous women
    and 151–152; inequities in 148–149;
    LGBTQIA+ families and 153–154
maternal mortality ratio (MMR)
    138–139; in low-income nations
    139–142; in Nepal 145–146
motherland 109

Namugerwa, Leah 82; *see also* climate
    justice

Parks, Rosa 127; *see also* Colvin,
    Claudette; racial justice
Peltier, Autumn 133–135
praxis 95, 185

queer theory 52

racial justice 43; *see also* Collins, Patricia
    Hill; Truth, Sojourner
racism, interpersonal 148; structural
    148
radical feminisms 52
radical hope 74, 186

social construct 34–37
solidarity 86–87, 123
systems of oppression 11, 22, 74,
    76–79, 83, 87

Thunberg, Greta 81–82; *see also*
    climate justice

transgender 36, 41, 153, 181, 187
transnational feminisms 1, 26, 187
Tripathi, Rukumani (Ruku) 144–147;
    *see also* maternal health
Truth, Sojourner 12, 44–46, 52, 89,
    112, 178
Tubman, Harriet 77, 112, 116–118, 160;
    *see also* racial justice
two spirit 34, 39

Underground Railroad 116, 118; *see
    also* racial justice; Tubman, Harriet
United Nations Sustainable
    Development Goals (SDG) 1, 18,
25–26; SDG 1 - No Poverty 136;
SDG 2 - Zero Hunger 91–92; SDG
3 - Good Health and Wellbeing
136, 138; SDG 5 - Gender Equality
18, 22, 25, 28, 33, 155–157; SDG
6 - Clean Water and Sanitation
131–132, 134–135; SDG 13 - Climate
Action 63
upstander 87

Watson, Emma 11, 47–48, 55, 57
womanism 70
Women's and Gender Studies
    (WGST) 3, 8–9, 30

For Product Safety Concerns and Information please contact our EU
representative GPSR@taylorandfrancis.com
Taylor & Francis Verlag GmbH, Kaufingerstraße 24, 80331 München, Germany

www.ingramcontent.com/pod-product-compliance
Ingram Content Group UK Ltd.
Pitfield, Milton Keynes, MK11 3LW, UK
UKHW031041080625
459435UK00013B/565